Con

GW00393980

Author's introduction

Walks for motorists? Certainly. Such a guide is needed. All motorists are not permanently locked in their steel boxes. Most enjoy a moderate walk and they have the best of both worlds. They can see and enjoy much more of the Lake District National Park's superb countryside.

Most previous general guides are of little use for motorists. The routes they describe are from "A" to "B". Anyone with personal transport wants a round walk to return to the start. ALL THE WALKS IN THIS GUIDE ARE FROM "A" TO "A", "A" BEING THE WALKER'S CAR.

Like a previous volume, this guide is not for athletes. It is for those who like a moderate walk with exceptional attractions. It is for photographers, amateur naturalists and for anyone interested in spending leisure time enjoying the natural beauty to the full. The walks can be enjoyed by all ages and by family parties.

This guide is not for fell walkers. Fine fell guides are already available. It is assumed that there are very many walkers who have no urge to meet the challenge of the wild high places. Mountain accident statistics for the area prove that too many walkers find themselves on the fells without the right equipment to face the rough ground, the strong winds and the sudden savage storms. From the valleys the fell paths can be seen easily and can offer a dangerous attraction. On the other hand the very delightful valley walks, the lake-shore paths and the ways to the viewpoints are not too apparent. They start at farm gates; hide up private-looking drives; and hide behind inns and churchyards. Yet they are rights of way for all to enjoy. This guide explains where some of the best can be found.

I am a fanatical fell-walker. But I also love the lush green valleys of the Lake District more than can be expressed. Most fell walkers do not know what they are missing in the valleys. They offer far more variety of scenery and some of the finest views. There is much more to see of nature. There are hundreds of miles of lower-level footpaths hardly discovered by modern generations; few of them are shown in current guides to the Lake District. This book is an attempt to introduce more countrygoers to the joys that they can offer.

It would have been possible to compile a roughly similar sort of guide to this, if one knew the Lake District very well, from an armchair. I have not done this. To compile this slim volume and select the right walks, the author has walked some 175 miles!

If some readers wonder why their favourite walk has been left out it should be remembered that some regard had to be given to the

LAKE DISTRICT WALKS FOR MOTORISTS
Northern Area

Warne Gerrard Guides for Walkers

Walks for Motorists Series

CHESHIRE WALKS

CHILTERNS WALKS
        Northern
        Southern

COTSWOLDS WALKS
        Northern
        Southern

EXMOOR WALKS

JERSEY WALKS

LAKE DISTRICT WALKS
        Central
        Northern
        Western

LONDON COUNTRYSIDE WALKS
        North West
        North East
        South West
        South East

GREEN LONDON WALKS
        (both circular and cross country)

MIDLAND WALKS

NORTH YORK MOORS WALKS
        North and East
        West and South

PEAK DISTRICT WALKS

PENDLESIDE AND BRONTE COUNTRY WALKS

SNOWDONIA WALKS
        Northern

SOUTH DOWNS WALKS

WYE VALLEY WALKS

YORKSHIRE DALES WALKS

FURTHER DALES WALKS

Long Distance and Cross Country Walks

WALKING THE PENNINE WAY

RAMBLES IN THE DALES

Warne Gerrard Guides for Walkers

LAKE DISTRICT

WALKS FOR MOTORISTS

NORTHERN AREA

John Parker

30 circular walks with 29 sketch maps
4 photographs by Geoffrey Berry

FREDERICK WARNE

Published by
Frederick Warne (Publishers) Ltd.
London

© Copyright 1972

First published 1972
Reprinted 1973
First revised edition 1974
Reprinted (twice) 1975
Second revised edition 1976
Reprinted 1976
Reprinted 1978
Third revised edition 1978
Reprinted 1979

The picture on the front cover shows Derwentwater and Skiddaw from Ashness, and is reproduced by permission of the National Trust. The back cover picture is of Grange-in-Borrowdale and was taken by Tom Parker. All the other pictures were taken by Geoffrey Berry.

Please let us know

Every care has been taken in the compilation of this book but the publishers cannot accept responsibility for any inaccuracies. But things change; paths are sometimes diverted; Concrete bridges replace wooden ones; stiles disappear. Please let the publishers know if you discover anything like this on your way.

ISBN 0 7232 2157 X

Printed by Galava Printing Co. Ltd., Nelson, Lancashire

problems of car parking and the need to provide a route suitable for all ages.

RIGHTS OF WAY

ALL THE WALKS DESCRIBED HERE ARE ON OFFICIAL RIGHTS OF WAY, OR PERMISSIVE FOOTPATHS, OR ON PUBLIC ACCESS AREAS. Some guides have caused trouble and distress to landowners and farmers as they have encouraged trespass and indirectly caused damage to walls and fences. THIS GUIDE DESCRIBES OFFICIALLY-DESIGNATED PATHS AND BRIDLEWAYS, THE RIGHT OF PASSAGE OVER WHICH CANNOT BE PROPERLY CHALLENGED. There is the proviso, however, that routes are legally changed from time to time by developments or road improvements, in which case the altered alignment should be signposted.

The rights are plain. The responsibilities should be recognised too. Right of passage across a farm field, for instance, does not mean a right to wander off the path to picnic. Grass is an important growing crop. It is damaged by trampling. Dogs, too, need to be kept under proper control. It is strongly recommended that every dog should be on a lead when passing through farmland. Even "harmless" dogs, if they are boisterous and playful among farm stock, can cause harm. Farmers have a right to put an unlocked gate across a right of way. Walkers have a responsibility, after opening such a gate, to close it behind them to prevent stock wandering. Litter—even sweet wrappings—should be taken back to the car.

When there is free public access, and one can wander at will off the path, this guide usually mentions it.

EQUIPMENT

A map is not strictly necessary if this guide is carried, as the routes are described in detail and sketch maps provided. All one needs to know is which is one's left hand, and which one's right! A one-inch to the mile tourist map, or one of the new Ordnance metric maps, however, adds interest and helps to identify points in distant prospects that are not mentioned. Such maps also show the local roads. See special note on page 9. A pocket-compass is not necessary either but it can add interest.

The most important item of equipment is footwear. But the comparatively expensive fell-walking boots are not needed here. Footwear above all should be well fitting and reasonably waterproof. Ideally, to prevent blistering they should be worn over woollen socks. Completely smooth soles can be a misery as they slide on wet stones and grass and waste energy. Clothing should be comfortable, and lightweight waterproofs should be carried.

Even if the intention is to be back at the car for a meal, some food should be packed in case you are delayed. Other, optional, equipment might include cameras, sketch pads, plant or bird identification books and binoculars. It goes without saying that kitchen sinks, transistor radios, newspapers, portable TV sets and the grinding worries of everyday modern life should be firmly left behind.

The best equipment of all is an eye to see everything afresh.

THE LAKE DISTRICT NATIONAL PARK AND THE NATIONAL TRUST

The whole of the Lake District from the A6. in the east to the coast of Cumbria in the west, is a National Park — 866 square miles. This does not mean that all this land belongs to the nation and you can wander on it at will. It means that it is a very specially protected area where any unsightly development is prevented. Its governing body — the National Park Planning Board — also has a duty to help the public to enjoy the amenities. It can, for instance, acquire land for public access and for car parks. It provides an Information Service, and the information centres can be found in some of the busier areas. Brockhole, the National Park Visitor Centre, is a house set among lovely gardens by the lake shore between Ambleside and Windermere. There is a permanent exhibition there with lectures and film shows illustrating all that the Lake District has to offer. It is well worth a visit.

The National Park also has a Warden Service. There are several professional wardens and a lot of weekend volunteers. They could be met on the footpaths and access areas described here and can be recognised by their armbands and badges, and their cars have screen stickers. They are there to encourage good behaviour; to enforce by-laws and the litter act; but their main function is to be friendly and helpful. They are "mobile information centres".

THE NATIONAL TRUST, on the other hand, in spite of what its title might suggest, has nothing to do with government. It is a private body entirely supported by voluntary contributions. It exists to acquire land and property of natural beauty and of historic importance; for their protection and for the public to enjoy. By great good fortune the NATIONAL TRUST is one of the largest landowners in the Lake District National Park. It owns fells, lakes and valleys and protects them for all time. Many of the farms are in NATIONAL TRUST ownership. The Trust also has information points in various parts of the Lake District.

The NATIONAL PARK PLANNING BQARD and the NATIONAL TRUST operate together in the Lake District for the public good.

THE COUNTRY CODE

Your walks can be marred if you cause trouble to farmers, landowners or fellow walkers. Unpleasant encounters can be avoided given a little common-sense and imagination. Some of these points have been mentioned but are so important that they are repeated.

LITTER IS OFFENSIVE AND DANGEROUS AND SHOULD NEVER BE LEFT. Children and the elderly are apt to be forgetful and they should be reminded of this.

Dogs, even normally harmless friendly dogs, should be properly controlled. A lead should be carried and used where necessary.

If closed gates are encountered, they should be closed after you.

The other points of the Country Code are a matter of common sense, too. Keep to the paths. Avoid damaging drystone walls. Beware against contaminating drinking water. Respect other people's property, privacy and right to enjoy peace and quiet. Guard against risk of fire—especially in or near woodland. Resist the temptation to uproot or damage plants, ferns, shrubs or trees.

Last, but not least, drive carefully, and walk carefully, on the narrow country roads.

USEFUL ADDRESSES

If a right of way is obstructed, it would be of service if the matter were reported, with precise details and location, as soon as possible. Footpaths are the responsibility of the local Highway Authority. Complaints may be sent to the Clerk, Cumbria County Council, Carlisle, Cumbria.

Other useful addresses:

Accommodation and Tourist Information: Cumbria Tourist Board, Ellerthwaite, Windermere, Cumbria.

National Park Information Service: District Bank House, High Street, Windermere, Cumbria.

The National Trust Broadlands, Borrans Road, Ambleside, Cumbria.

The National Park Visitor Centre Brockhole, Windermere.

The Friends of the Lake District is the local preservation society. The Secretary, 27 Greenside, Kendal.

The Lake District Naturalists' Trust concerns itself with the local preservation of nature and owns several reserves. The Secretary, Bleak House, Park Road, Windermere, Cumbria.

Ordnance Survey Maps

1:50,000 series. All walks in this book are on sheet no. 90.

1:25,000 Outdoor Leisure Maps. All walks except no. 14 are on 'The English Lakes North West sheet and North East sheet; Walks 1 to 13, 15, 17 and 18 are on the NW sheet, Walks 16 and 19 to 30 on the NE sheet.

1-inch to the mile 'Lake District' Tourist map. All walks are on this sheet.

This is an excellent walk for a clear day as the views from it are superb. The walk has a unique merit — unless there is a deluge dry feet are absolutely guaranteed, as the route is entirely on forest roads. These are not legal rights of way; but the Forestry Commission allows walkers to use their roads provided that one takes care about the risk of starting fires, and no litter is left. So smokers in particular should beware. To begin with the walk is a longish climb — for about an hour, allowing longer for short legs and short wind. But the effort — nowhere exceptional — is very amply rewarded with the beautiful views over Derwentwater and Bassenthwaite Lake. This is a photographer's dream.

At the moment the Forestry Commission are completely changing their attitude to the question of public access to woodlands. The taxpayers are in fact being encouraged to take an interest in the activities of the Commission and facilities are being provided for them to see more. At the time of writing experiments are being made with nature walks based on a small new car park at Mitre House Mill. You are recommended to park at the forest entrance a little north of Long Close farm. This is a wide entrance with parking space at its foot — but of course you must not park so as to obstruct the Commission's vehicles. You should leave room for a large timber lorry — or a fire engine — to get by. To find this entrance take the A591 out of Keswick — that is the Bothel and Carlisle road. Four minor roads leave this road, on the right, the last one doubling back sharply after two and a half miles. Long Close is shortly after this, on the left. There is a small lay-by on the right which you should pass, then get ready to turn — this is a fairly fast and potentially dangerous road. The forest entrance is then soon seen branching off on the right.

Leaving the car, walk up the forest road towards the gate. The wood at the fringe is a good mixture with hardwoods. The preservation of this type of growth around the edges of large forests is in accordance with modern forestry practice. Large unbroken plantings of dark conifers can spoil landscape. In this case there are some wild cherries and some copper beech with the common species. Go through the stile. There are some horse-chestnuts, and as the larches start on the left there is a handsome Noble Fir. Flower spotters will enjoy identifying the species along the road-sides.

The track zig-zags. There is an open area just beyond a little group of Scots Pines on the right. Ignore the right branch road at this point and continue left on the well-surfaced road. You are now

10

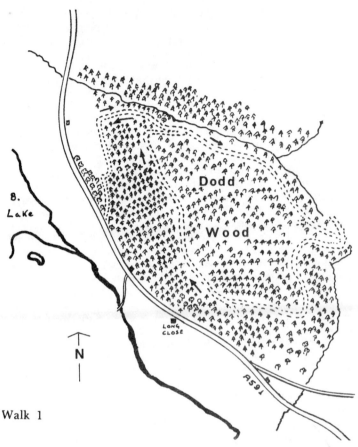

8.
Lake

Dodd

Wood

LONG
CLOSE

N

A591

Walk 1

among the plantings proper—Douglas Firs. At fork continue left on
the lower level surfaced road. A view opens up left over the foot of
Bassenthwaite. Further on as the road curves right there is a view
over the head of the lake. The road then curves in towards the
mountain. A fork is reached, the right hand road doubling back;
keep right on. You are now among more recent plantings of Sitka
Spruce. Both Douglas and Sitka are trees of the North Americas and
grow well in Britain. There are soon larches on the left, and here
and there is an odd planting of Western Hemlock. This is
another American tree much planted nowadays in Britain as it
tolerates some shade and is very useful for underplanting. The
growing shoot of this tree is bent over and this is one way of picking it
out. The beeches here are very poor from a forester's point of view.
There are far too many side-branches and this is probably due to bad

stock. Deer in this area are not as common as in the south of the Lake District, but some roe-deer damage to the young trees can be seen in places. The roe-bucks mark their territory by scraping the bark off the young trees with their antlers.

Another track joins from the right. Carry right on. The plantings are now somewhat mixed as you get high, and the growth is somewhat less successful. You are now at about 1,200 feet. (This news will not be at all surprising to the faint-hearted.) This is really heath and heather country, though you may enjoy some wild raspberries about here. The road bends left to a T-junction. Turn right and continue to climb. At long last the road levels and you begin to descend among spruce trees. Down a fire-break to the left is a bird's-eye view over Keswick. Just after this there is a view over Derwentwater. A road joins from the left; continue right. After this there is a view left and you can see the low-level plain between Derwentwater and Bassenthwaite Lake. The indications are that at one time the two lakes were one but became separated by silting. After prolonged and heavy rain in fact, even nowadays, the lakes again become one. The views are now excellent and it is hoped that the Forestry Commission will not allow them to become obscured by tree growth. Way over to the left of Derwentwater one can see Helvellyn. To the right of Derwentwater Cat Bells can be seen end on, with the valley of Newlands to its right. Dale Head and Hindscarth are at its top. If the weather is clear you should see the Scafells and Great Gable behind these.

A lane comes in from the left, and a grass one goes off right; continue right on. The road begins to gain a little height and then left there is a wonderful view over Bassenthwaite Lake. At the head of the lake opposite is a group of white buildings among which is the Swan Hotel. Above on the fell side a spot of white will show. This is "The Bishop", a rock with the shape of such a dignitary, standing in a pulpit. By tradition this is occasionally white-washed. Reward to the worthy who performs this chore is a drink "on the house"; though the climb with a bucket of whitewash is a bit hazardous there is no shortage of volunteers.

As a rise is breasted there is a magnificent view over the whole of Bassenthwaite. The road loops back into the fell side. A T-junction is joined. Turn left. You are now on the road back to the entrance.

This delightful walk has the very unusual merit for the Lake District of being practically a level one. Those who have been brought up on Beatrix Potter tales should recognise this area too as Mrs Tiggy-Winkle's territory; and the walk takes the path which that famous character must have waggled along; with her print gown tucked up and a large apron over her striped petticoat, and her nose going sniffle sniffle sniffle and her eyes going twinkle twinkle. Somewhere along the hill side should be the little wooden door into her tiny house, and of course Little Town is where Lucy lived. Those who have not read Beatrix Potter will think the author has taken leave of his senses, but they will enjoy this easy walk all the same!

Take the A594 west out of Keswick and at Portinscale (1½ miles) turn left to go down towards the west side of Derwentwater. Keeping left at the road junctions on the way continue for about two miles then up a short steep hill over a cattle grid. Then immediately afterwards turn right down the narrow road. There is a public car park a little way along it on the left — Gutherscale. Park here.

Walk on along the road. There is shortly a view right over the foot of the valley (Newlands) towards Bassenthwaite Lake. The dominating fell over on the right is Grisedale Pike. Just as you are reaching the gate across the road, take the grassy track which leaves the road on the left. As you go on up this track you will have a view of the valley head, and over it, in the distance, Red Pike which overlooks Buttermere and Crummock Water. The large hump at the actual valley head is Robinson (2,417 feet). Hindscarth (2,385 feet) is on the left of this. Nearer, on the left, is a spur of Maiden Moor called High Crags, and all along on the left is Cat Bells. Whenever the path appears to fork, keep to the more prominent track which goes forward more or less on the level, with a wall on the right. All the time you should be admiring the valley on the right. Note how the scattered trees make the scene.

At the end of this track you approach the waste heaps of an old mine — Yewthwaite. This has not been extensively worked in this century but from the eighteenth century it produced lead, iron pyrites, and cerussite (a carbonate of lead). At its peak it was making a profit for its owner of £3,000 per annum, which was real money at that time. It declined when the ancient mine of Goldscope higher up the valley enjoyed a new, and profitable, lease of life. Nothing much can be seen now of Yewthwaite's workings except the debris. One of the entrances went into a level above the waste heap on the left but the roof has collapsed.

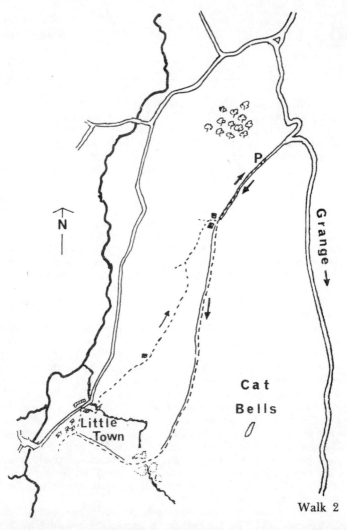

Walk 2

The track goes through the workings (note the old cobbled section which was part of the yard) and then it goes off to the right following round a wall. The beck down from the left disappears into the waste heaps to emerge lower down. The pretty little village of Little Town is seen on the right. It is approached by following the track round, and doubling back on a zig-zag. The scene is added to at this point by the wind-swept grove of larch. Although Beatrix Potter lived far off at Sawrey, and at Troutbeck, she visited Little Town and wrote and sketched here, staying at the farm where she placed her character Lucy.

Go through the buildings on the macadam road, but directly after them take the track on the right which goes between walls. On the right at the end of the first wall is the shattered remnant of a cherry tree which is still clinging to life. Follow the track on through the gate and over a little foot-bridge. Go through the gate at the end of this hedged and walled path, towards the gate by the house. Go through the gate and follow the track onwards, a pleasant walk across a field. When you come to the old stone gate post on the left, on the right is a broken fragment of an ash still clinging to life. The ash tree behind it is hollow too. Many of the ash trees around the old farms here are hollow because the tops of the trees were cut off in winter so that the hungry sheep could feed on the twigs. The line of gnarled hawthorn trees is the remains of an old hedge. Go through the wooden kissing-gate. Now the path is indistinct, but continue on, keeping the hedge on your left.

When the hedge finishes move over across the field towards the right and follow the line of another hedge to a gate. Go through the gate to pick up a more distinct track alongside a hedge to another gate. Then go on through another gate towards the farm — Skelgill. Then go through the buildings onto the macadam road and turn right. Go through the gate, and onto the road, left, beyond. You are soon back at the car park at Gutherscale.

Prominent from most places in Keswick is the green steep-sided hill on the north-east side of the town. A look is usually enough to anyone except a dedicated fell-walker. It is, as they say in the Lake District "brant", which means an eye-popping lung-bursting slope. In fact, however, there is an easy path to the top; it creeps up the back way and was much loved by Victorian tourists. If the stern-minded walkers of yesteryear could do the walk in tight stays and stiff collars most readers of this book should be able to make it too. The reward is a splendid view over Keswick at the head of Derwentwater and the hills beyond.

Park in Keswick. Walk up Station Street past the Art Gallery and little Museum (worth a visit) and then just before the Keswick Hotel take the road to the right (Brundholme Road). Follow the road on and round the left-hand curve. Just after this there is no footpath, so take care. Continue on along this road by the residential estate. At the end of one of the roads leading into the estate is a post box, on the left. Just after this there is a lane on the right running up between fences and old hedges. Go up this. Cross the bridge over the A66. Go through the gate beyond the cottage and up between a fence on the left and a line of ash trees on the right. Go through an old gateway and avoid wetness by scrambling up on the right of the path. Follow along the line of the fence under sycamore trees. (If you cannot recognise a sycamore think of a maple leaf, the badge of Canada, which everyone knows. The sycamore is a relative with a slightly similar leaf. Introduced long ago into Britain it is now one of our commonest trees.) There is a view left over Bassenthwaite Lake and the flat green alluvial plain which separates it from Derwentwater.

Cross the footbridge at the zig-zag then go right along the edge of the wood—mainly Sitka spruce and beech. There is a line of pines and larch, right. After passing the trees you go into the open on a zig-zag. There is a view now over to Skiddaw. Go round the fell side following the fence, and when the path begins to level out look for a sharp turn upwards on the right on a grassy path. Take this. It soon zig-zags left, then right at an old gateway. A view over Keswick opens up, to the lake head. There is a wet gully obstructing the path. Go round it above it. When the path ends at an edge overlooking Keswick the way is left, for the summit by the dead trees. Rest on the summit and enjoy the prospect. Always prominent on the Derwentwater scene is the small peaked fell on its west side. This is Cat Bells. It is a fell very tempting to walkers—yet strangely has a very high accident record because of its steep slippery sides. The sharp pike on the fell over to its right is Causey.

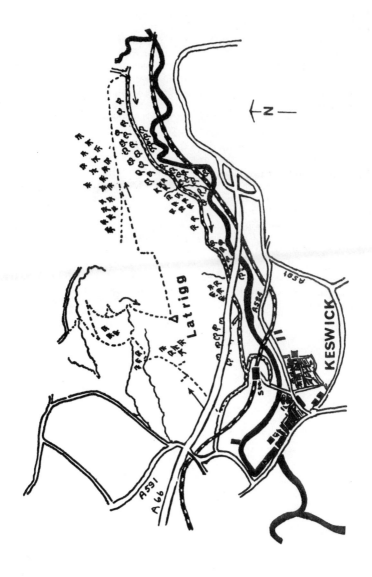

Walk 3

Continue on, in the same direction as before, to beyond the summit. Blencathra is ahead, end on. Way over in the background to the right is the Helvellyn range. You reach a stile. Cross it and turn left to follow the fence. (The field here is often full of wild pansies in July and August. Admire them but do not pluck!) The path here is indistinct. At fence corner turn right and follow this fence. At the next fence corner walk on in the same direction. Just before the way is blocked by a fence turn left to the gate. Go through the gate and follow the edge of the wood — a larch and beech plantation. Continue on beyond it, on a track. Descending by a wood, go through a gate onto a macadam lane. Turn right to follow it. You are soon walking into a typical natural wood with oak and birch and an undercover of hazels. Nearly all the dead birches have growing on them the rough white fungus known as the "razor strop" as its leathery surface might be used for that purpose. There are also many woodpecker holes in the dead trees and in spring and early summer you should hear the "laughter" of the 'peckers. Plant growth is limited to some extent under the heavy tree cover, but there are always foxgloves, wood sage, and enchanter's nightshade. Sallow bushes take over the wet places.

After a curve and a dip in the road you are through new plantings and among elders and ash. The new larch and spruce will soon grow to screen off the road below. Cross the bridge over the A66. As you approach the buildings there is a mixture of trees including a tall silver fir and then some old oaks. Children will also spot "conker trees", the horse chestnuts. You join a T junction. Turn left to regain your starting point.

At one time every visitor to Keswick had to climb up the little hill known as Castle Head to see, for very little effort, a view that some higher summits cannot boast. Modern tourists are more inclined to drive out of Keswick to find the views but this should really not be missed. The walk can finish at Friar's Crag, the famous lake shore viewpoint to which almost everyone goes and you can, if you wish, continue down the lake shore southwards to the first landing-stage at Ashness gate to catch the service motor-boat back.

Nearly all the good things around Keswick and in Borrowdale belong to the National Trust. The history of the Trust is very much bound up with the protection of this area. Almost the whole of the shore of Derwentwater, half the lake, and the finest viewpoints are "in Trust". Praise be. Almost the whole of this walk is on Trust land.

From the town centre, having parked the car, leave the market place with its Moot Hall (now an Information Centre run by the National Park Information Service with the Keswick Publicity Association) and go up St. John Street past the spired church. When this street comes to the foot of a steep rise, Springs Road is on the right. Go down this road and before reaching the turn in this road look for the narrow path between a hedge and fence on the right. Go along this, through the kissing-gate and up the steps on the left, then go right between two big oaks and upwards on the broad path. The wood is of interest because, unlike many woods in the area, it is not grazed by sheep and therefore the trees can reproduce by seedlings. As you follow the path you will see that ash tree seedlings have grown thickly; and sycamore, hazel and some beech and elm are also coming up. Strangely, oak seedlings are less common, which suggests that the acorn crop is largely taken by birds—wood pigeons and jays eat them greedily. But there might also be other reasons. Ash, hazel and certainly beech can tolerate more shade. There is an undercover of enchanter's nightshade and deadnettle; raspberries and black-berries also though not much fruit is produced in these shade conditions. Go upwards by four yew trees—two either side and past the firs to the summit. The view is a pleasant surprise. It is very well photographed and the Scots pines, typical on such an exposed site, frame the scene nicely. An indicator on a plinth points out the surrounding peaks and gives their names.

Descend the way you came to the top of the steps above the kissing-gate and turn sharp right to a broad path through a thicket. This passes a crag face. There is a seat by a fine silver fir. There are two more beyond the seat and a fine oak. Here, in contrast to what we

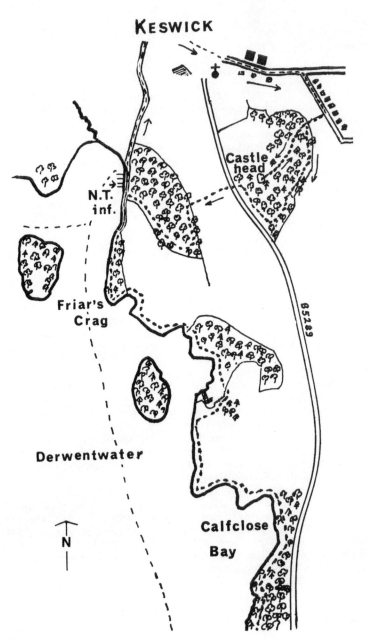

KESWICK

Castle head

N.T. inf.

Friar's Crag

Derwentwater

N

Calfclose Bay

B5289

Walk 4

saw earlier, oak seedlings are doing well on both sides of the path, with holly. Bear right and go alongside the road on the edge of the wood. Presently, looking across the road, you will see some steps. Go down some steps to cross the road and go with care to the steps on the other side. Descend them and go on to the path between the fence and hedge. Go through a kissing-gate into another wood. At fork turn right. Just here there is a varied mixture of natural regeneration of oak, beech, holly, hawthorn, sycamore and rowan. Further on ash seems to be winning again.

You then descend to the "promenade" by the boat landings. On the right there is a National Trust Information Centre and sales counter. On the left is Friar's Crag. On the way there you pass a memorial tablet to Canon Rawnsley. This remarkable man of energy, the incumbent of Crosthwaite Church in Keswick, was associated with many causes, but he is specially remembered for his work towards the foundation of the National Trust, the preservation of the Lake District and the defence of rights of way. The Friar's Crag land was purchased by subscribers in his memory. On reaching the crag there is a memorial to another Lake District preservationist —John Ruskin, who was associated with the area for most of his life. Author, philosopher, art critic and no mean artist himself; his voice had to be listened to at a time when countryside conservation was becoming a world-wide issue.

If you wish, you can continue the walk along the side of the Lake for over a mile by way of Calfclose Bay to the landing stage at Ashness Gate where you can board a boat. This might be one returning to the Keswick landings, or you could pick up the boat going on her outward journey and go right round the lake. A time-table is displayed at the landing.

This is a "must" for visitors to the Keswick area. The whole walk can be taken at once, or it can be taken in two parts. The former is recommended – but take a long time over it as you can sit by the lake shore in several lovely places; or take the whole walk at a very leisurely speed.

Take the A66 Portinscale road out of Keswick. Go left at Portinscale and through the village. At 1¾ miles turn left, heading for Grange-in-Borrowdale. On reaching steep section and cattle grid, turn left, and one mile further on, where the road begins to overlook the lake, park the car. There is a space to the left, with an old rough track going to the bay below; or there is parking space in the old gravel cuttings on the roadside to the right.

Above the road you will see an old terraced track running parallel to it. Join it by one of the paths, and continue walking on it towards the head of the lake (the direction in which you were travelling previously). There are fine views, left. As you go on look back towards the foot of the lake. Among the slates at your feet the parsley-like fern is an alpine; the Alpine Polypody. The terraced path climbs a little and there are splendid views over the woods of Manesty, particularly colourful in spring and autumn. There are fine views over the lake. The best viewpoint is by the stone seat – which you will reach – erected to the memory of Sir Hugh Walpole. He wrote best-selling novels, including Rogue Herries which has a local setting, and lived in the house just below.

The track drops to a corner of a large wood and follows the wall. It is here a narrow footpath, but after the wall finishes, it widens again to a track and continues to descend. It goes through a gate and the road is joined. Continue in same direction. Before reaching the buildings on the left there is a gate on the left, with a track. It should be signposted "Footpath to Lodore". Go on this track by the stream and go over the bridge. The track becomes less distinct as a path over damp ground. Go forward, picking the driest way, veering right towards the lake where a better path will again be picked up. Go through the kissing-gate and on path beyond. Go through the fence gap and, where the path forks, take the left hand one. It becomes less distinct, but should go on bearing right to the wooded promontory. If you walk this way in May or June there is a good show of wild flowers, including bluebells, wood anemonies (a white flower), and look for the tiny bright blue flower – the milkwort and the pink lousewort.

At the end of the promontory the path can be more clearly seen, as a green one. In the bog there is cotton grass. The path bends left

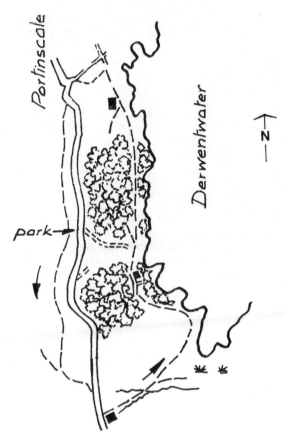

Walk 5   *Grange & Borrowdale*

past a wooden seat. Go through wooden kissing-gate into the wood.
The path is some way from the shore, but this is an access area and
you can wander along the lake edge. The path crosses several little
wooden bridges. Watch for red squirrels. The path joins a macadam
lane near a bungalow. When it forks, turn left, go through gate and
then bear right past the garage towards the lake shore. Go along the
lake shore by this bay, cross the stile and continue on the lake shore.
(Your car is above you at this point if you are cutting the walk
in two.)

    You walk along sand and gravel from some old mine workings.
You go through a little pinewood and past a public landing. You now
continue by the lake shore by a very pretty hard woodland area —
Brandelhow Park. There are hereabouts some fine tree specimens

including a tall straight Douglas Fir by the side of the path, and another farther on. At the end of the wood go through the kissing-gate and skirt the edge of the field. A wooden stile is crossed at the far end and we are again in woods by the shore. You go by the side of a bay, over a stile and by the side of a field. You then follow a fence back. At the end of the fence turn right over a wooden walkway. Cross a little beck and go on on well-defined track. Go through the iron kissing-gate, then turn down to the lake shore again. Go on along the lake shore. At the next bay your way turns left and goes through an iron kissing-gate. Cross the lane and go through another kissing-gate opposite. Climb the bank bearing left, go left upwards following the wall. Go through another iron kissing-gate to join the path alongside the road, left. Go through gate and turn left following the fence up. Cross the macadam road and go up the terrace path opposite, continuing in the same direction. You are soon above the road again with fine views towards Keswick, and over the lake to Ashness Woods. Skiddaw and Blencathra are also prominent away to the left. The higher you go the more magnificent the view. The path then begins to lose height, but still with fine views, and you are eventually back at your starting point.

This walk offers splendid high-level views over Derwentwater and, for contrast, falls to the lake shore by way of a forest trail. There is a climb at the beginning, but the path is not rough. Given reasonable footwear — that is with a good tread on the soles — anyone can manage the walk with ease.

The walk starts at the large car park at Great Wood, one and a half miles from Keswick on the Borrowdale road, and to the left of the road. The entrance has a restricted head room, so if you have a tall vehicle (eg minibus, dormobile) start the walk at Watendlath Road car park which lies a little way along the minor road going towards Ashness. Leave the car park, cross the road, and enter to lake shore land through a kissing-gate. Turn left. The lake shore here is in the care of the National Trust and there are some fine trees, particularly pine in the immediate vicinity. Over in the lake there is the smaller island called Rampsholme and beyond it the larger one of St. Herbert's island. As you continue along the lake shore you reach a point where crags steepen. Here there are several paths and you can take your choice. If the water is low it might be as well to walk by the lake edge. Take your time if you go by the crag and pick your route carefully; watch for tree roots. When you reach a landing-stage leave the path for the road. Cross it with care and go up the Watendlath Road past the small car park. If you have not previously been to the bridge, ahead, do so, and go just up the beck bank beyond it to see the view over Derwentwater with the bridge in the foreground. However our route goes on just before the bridge. There is an old gateway and near it a path going up the fell side on the left. The path climbs through bracken, and as you gain height there is a fine view left. The path passes over grass and rock and bears left. There are views over Derwentwater and towards Bassenthwaite Lake. The path steepens under a bent ash tree and then the way is less distinct. The direction is forward and left and the path can be picked up as it gains height less steeply. Later it levels off and gains height gradually. There are some even more splendid views. However, nearer the summit of the fell a shoulder of land obscures the immediate view over the lake.

Another track is joined; follow it left on a pleasant grassy track. The track narrows and curves round a cove, Cat Gill. The path widens and begins to leave the lake slightly and climb. Cross a beck by the stepping stones, and pass on to an open fell through heather patches. When a wall is reached follow it up slightly and then go over a stile and along the path beyond. The summit gives a bird's-eye

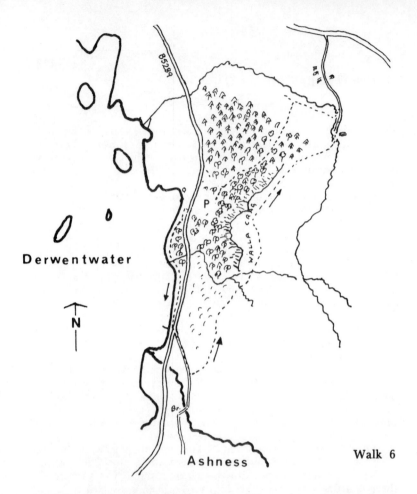

Derwentwater

N

Ashness

Walk 6

view of Keswick. Skiddaw is behind, and Blencathra on its right. Go to cairn. There is an extensive view in all directions. If it is clear, Scafell Pike and Great Gable can be seen well over to the left as you face the lake.

Pick up the path leading on from the cairn to the fence and follow the fence down, taking care on slippery rocks (and watching the barbed wire lest it tear your clothes.) Go over the stile, at the corner, and continue on to follow the wall. Start to descend and bear right towards a broad grassy track. Follow the wall ahead. After undulations the broad path descends on steep grass which can be slippery. Join a hard track and bear left. Go over a stile and continue down. Cross the footbridge and join the macadam road. A road joins from the right, near Rakefoot. Continue on. If you look over the wall on the left you will soon see a little footbridge. This is reached through a gate on the left. Cross the footbridge and turn right, under hazelnut trees. When the path forks continue on the right-hand one. Cross the stile. (Beware barbed wire). Cross another stile and at this point turn sharp left and head for the wood. Go over the stile into it and forward through the bracken.

Go down a narrow path between larch trees. The path widens and there is an iron ladder stile. Go over this or through the gate. Eventually the path comes to a cross-roads. Go straight across. The path is poor at first but gets better farther on. Go over a stile, then descend on the track which eventually rejoins the car park. Larches are soon broken by hazels and pines, and you are on a forest trail in Great Wood. This is a National Trust property. Eventually the path comes to a cross-roads. Go straight across. The path is poor at first but gets better farther on. Go over a stile, then left. You are on a green track which comes to the Borrowdale road at an old gateway. Cross the road with care and go through the kissing-gate opposite.

Those who appreciate the Lake District landscape should not miss seeing the great "classic" views, the prospect over Derwentwater with Ashness Bridge in the foreground being one of them.

One of the most photographed views in Britain, it has appeared on more calendars, greetings cards, tea trays, chocolate boxes and gift-shop ware than any other! Popularity might put some people off it. It should not. It remains excellent, and the only thing that could disappoint a photographer might be to see a car, parked by some unfeeling and inconsiderate motorist, by the roadside slap in the middle of the viewfinder.

A second classic is "Surprise View"; the open vista over Derwent-water that hits the traveller when northbound from Watendlath. It is dramatic in the extreme. The cliff below one's feet is so steep that one has the sensation of flight; and through the gap in the ring of fell walls is a view way over to Bassenthwaite Lake.

Of all the Lake District waterfalls, the falls of Lodore are the most famed. During the district's romantic period (when one could hardly move for poets, artists and authors) no tour was complete without a visit to them.

Yet here is a walk that combines all these attractions in a feast of beauty, for Nature has put them close together, and a round walk is easily achieved on good paths. A clear day is best — otherwise the views are lost and they are the reason for the walk. Ideally, it should be a clear day after heavy rain so that the falls can be seen at their dramatic best, but this might be too much to hope for. In any case the walk is worth doing. It is mainly through mixed woodland.

The walk starts at the public car park at Kettlewell Common. Take the Borrowdale road from Keswick. After two and a half miles there is a road junction left, then the road approaches close to the lake shore. Watch then for the car park on the right in a partly-wooded promontory.

Having parked, leave the car park by the entrance and turn left along the road. After a few yards there is a gap in the wall into the National Trust wood. Go through this gap and join the path, right, through the woods. Shortly after joining it the path bears left by a beck, then crosses a little footbridge over it. Go forward across a little beck. A waterfall may be heard on the left. This is a small and attractive steep fall but the approach to it is uninviting and slippery. Continue on through the wood. The path rises and goes by an old broken moss-covered wall before going closer to the road. On approaching a wall boundary of the Lodore Hotel land, the path

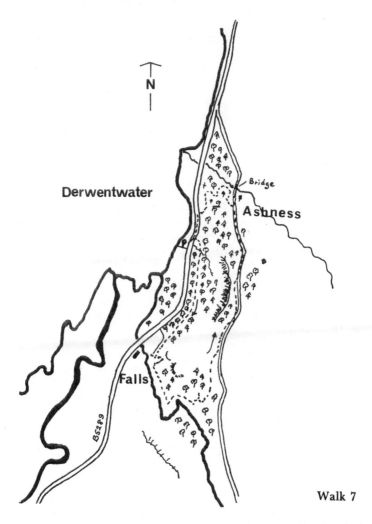

N

Derwentwater

Bridge

Ashness

Falls

BS289

Walk 7

goes inwards again, follows the wall for a distance, then heads for Lodor Falls which can probably be heard thundering away ahead.

On reaching the falls turn right towards the hotel to reach the best viewpoint for the lower part of them. (There are other good viewpoints from the beck sides higher, but if you seek them out take very great care over wet rock.)

Return to the footpath where you left it and go upwards with the beck on your right. Very shortly you will see a zig-zag start off to the left. Take this. The "zig" ends at a rock face, then there is a "zag" right. When this path reaches a fallen oak tree, look right for a pleasant view over Derwentwater with Skiddaw in the background. The path reaches the upper part of the falls, and there is a natural platform where you can view them. The woodland below was mainly broadleaf trees, but as you climb higher there are some European larch. The crags to the left above you are very awesome, but attractively clothed in green moss, ferns and foxgloves, with wood sage, honeysuckle, ivy, bilberry and heather. The path reaches some rock steps which some people may find a little awkward. Take your time over them.

The path climbs steadily and easily all the way. Ignore the lesser paths which branch off it to the right towards the beck. Eventually you will reach a gap in a broken wall. Continue on along more level ground through the wood. The path curves left. A Y-junction is eventually reached. The path on the left apparently goes towards the edge of a crag. The right one is to be taken. This is better defined and rises slightly, with the beck still running to its right. Another junction is reached. Turn left along the path which is built up; it runs at a sharp angle and there is a small holly tree at its foot. It presently bends sharply right, eventually running less distinctly through bracken, but immediately afterwards joining a hard, very well defined, footpath. Turn left, and keep on this hard path. It bears right to join a macadam road. Turn left to follow this road, on a course parallel to it.

Soon this road makes a closer approach to the crags on the left. You are approaching "Surprise View". There is a surfaced clearing on the right and just after this the view is a few steps to the left. Do not venture too near the edge! The view is magnificent. Derwentwater, with Keswick at the foot of Skiddaw, is to the right. Bassenthwaite is on to the left. Directly opposite is the fell of Catbells, and to the left of that is Maiden Moor. It may be possible to see the top of Great Gable in the distance to the left. Grisedale Pike is behind and to the right of Catbells. The Grasmoor range is behind to the left. Where the river Derwent flows into the lake you can see large gravel beds. These are built up during every flood, and there has been a tendency, over many hundreds of years, for all the lakes to become smaller and more shallow. For some time after the last ice age, which made the lakes, Derwentwater and Bassenthwaite Lake were probably a single large lake.

Follow the road down and forward again, joining it to go through a gateway. The road crosses a bridge and a cattle grid. When you then pass through another gateway, a barn will be seen on the right, and just below this is Ashness Bridge. For the best viewpoint over Derwentwater,. cross the bridge and turn right up the beck side before looking back. Though the view is familiar, here is a case where familiarity can never breed contempt. Photographers may decide that the best view is got by standing in the beck!

The way down is by public roads and is not too pleasant if there is traffic in abundance, particularly on the main Borrowdale road at the bottom. All, or nearly all, of this can happily be avoided on permissive footpaths. Turn back up the road the way you have come. Pass the barn again and the gateway, and a clearing is seen on the right. Walk into this and on the right again is a stile over a fence. Cross the stile, and follow the footpath downwards through the plantation. This reaches another stile at the foot, by the beck side. Cross the stile, then bear left on the footpath away from the beck. There is a portion of the path which is not too clear, but as you descend it is more easily seen, as it crosses under holly trees. Just after the hollies ignore the path to the right, but descend left. The path zig-zags under more holly trees. Do not worry if the paths are indistinct. The object is to lose height without wandering over the fence-line which comes down on the right.

Soon the roadside wall is approached, and there are beds of the Lesser Periwinkle (Vinca minor) with the small pleasantly blue flowers in bloom from April to July. The plant is uncommon, and protected by the National Trust by-laws. Do not uproot any! A path should be seen running parallel to the road; turn left along it. This soon ends up at a narrow gateway. Go through it with care onto the road, cross the road with even more care, and follow it on to the left and you are soon back at the car park where you started.

This is a good walk for strollers, loafers and folk who like to throw stones in water. It offers some very fine views but its disadvantage is that the return journey follows the same route (though one can see the scene both ways.) Its advantage is that the walk is almost completely level.

Park in Kettlewell car park (see walk 7). Leave the car park and walk carefully left for a short distance until you see a gap in the wall on your right. Go through this and join the path to the right. Go on through the trees and cross a footbridge. Follow the path on through this mossy wood until the way is close to the road. A wall is then reached, the wall of the grounds belonging to the Lodore Hotel. Turn right here and re-join the main road through a gate. Go carefully left along the road until the pavement is reached on the other side of the road. Walk along here until you come to a stile just after a gate. There should be a sign "Footpath to Manesty". Go onto this path and across a bridge and along the green path beyond. This leads onto wooden plank-walks over the wet ground (Note: if someone is coming from the opposite direction there is a specially constructed passing-place in the middle.) Go left round some oak trees to join another plank-walk. Left from here is a good view up the tree-cloaked jaws of Borrowdale.

You then reach the end of Great Bay on Derwentwater, with fine views over the lake. Follow the bay round until you come to a pine-crowned promontory. There is a splendid view from here. The woods are very fine, and are cared for by the National Trust. There are pines and larch and oak, and a population of red squirrels. You may not see these shy creatures but you may find fir cones that have been chewed down to the core, for the animals eat the seeds. Unless vandals have been around there should be water lillies in bloom in the summer. All the shore here is public access land and you may stay as long as you care to.

On the return journey you will see facing you Shepherd's Crag which is very popular with climbers. The most prominent climb is the one on the left. Here is Brown Slabs where the novices learn the sport, and with a pair of binoculars you may have an entertaining time watching them. Continue the walk by the outward route.

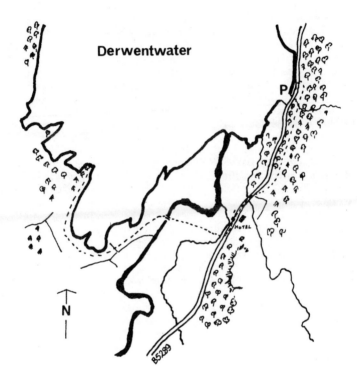

Derwentwater

P

HOTEL

B5289

N

Walk 8

Although the mileage is not great, the steepness to the 980-feet summit has to be taken slowly. This walk is not, repeat *not* for walkers with a "poor head for heights". Strong footwear is needed. Lone walkers should leave clear word with someone about the route they are taking as sprained ankles are not an impossibility on the steep slate paths.

This is a walk for views, and in misty or rainy weather the effort would be wasted. Having given these warnings let it be said that the view from the summit is breathtaking and superior to many view-points a good deal higher. It is a central platform in the centre of a highly dramatic amphitheatre. Photographers will go mad with delight — particularly in spring or autumn when the Borrowdale colours are at their best.

Drive up Borrowdale to the hamlet of Grange (4 miles), cross the lovely bridge and park. Walk into the hamlet. Just before reaching the little church, on the right, there is a lane on the left between a building and a farm wall. (Signposted "Public Footpath to Castle Crag & Rosthwaite".) Go down this lane. As you go forward Castle Crag an be seen ahead and an ascent of it might seem impossible, yet the track is an old road and is well defined. Go on through a gate. The way then goes close to the river at a point where the river bends sharply left. Ignore the quarry road right, and the path left with the river's bend. Go right on, over a little slate bridge. The path begins to climb, a beck crosses it, then you go through another gate. The rugged ridge above on the right is Eel Crags.

The way then becomes steeper and rougher. You cross a culverted beck under the crags of Castle Crag. At a point where the path again crosses the beck right, turn left up the grass bank to follow the stream for a short distance, then bear left up the steepness towards the wall. In the wet ground hereabouts, butterwort grows. This is a plant which feeds on insects, trapping them in its glossy narrow leaves, which then roll in towards the centre. In mid-May the flower is rather pretty — like a small violet on a long upright stalk. A look back down Derwentwater to Skiddaw is impressive. Cross the wall by a collapsed stile. The path here is very steep. There is a seat on the right under a crag with a memorial plaque. A wooden ladder stile is reached — a bad one when this was written. Over this, turn right immediately and continue ascending. (There are several routes from now on. Some of the short cuts are terrible. Follow the recommended route.) The path zig-zags; a grassy area is then reached with a cairn on it. Go to the cairn then go left by the zig-zags up the slates — with care. There are good views up Borrowdale — stop to admire

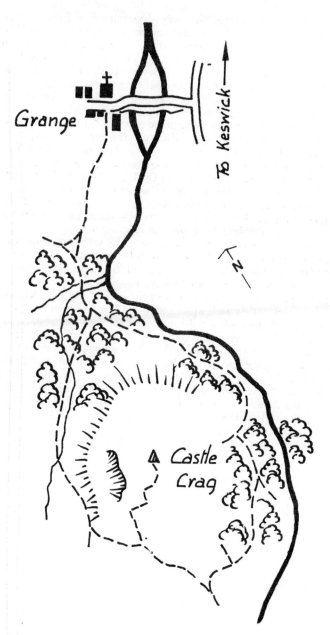

Grange

To Keswick →

N

Castle
Crag

Walk 9

them or you could trip! The valley bearing left is Stonethwaite. The crag standing in it is Eagle Crag and to the left of it is the old way for the pack-ponies to Grasmere. To the right of this valley Glaramara crowns the head of Borrowdale. Beyond that to its right is the end of the Scafells range — Great End. Behind that can be seen the little conical top of Scafell Pike, the highest point in England.

At the top of the slate zig-zags you pass by the rim of a quarry and you are soon at the summit. The view is splendid. Over Derwentwater is Skiddaw and to its right Blencathra (Saddleback). The tree-clad eminence across the valley on the right is King How and Grange Fell. In the background to the right of this is the Helvellyn range. Up Borrowdale now is a good view of the Scafell range, and to its right can be seen Great Gable. Little can be seen of the earthworks of the British fort which crowned Castle Crag. Erosion and the extensive quarrying activity have taken toll. The fort must have been almost impregnable anyway in such a position, and the typical ditch and earth wall might have been almost superfluous.

The only safe way off the summit is the way you came up. Make sure you pick your way down correctly by the slate zig-zags. Do not be tempted too far to the right. When you find yourself at the cairn on the grassed area again, go forward to the wall. Behind one of the pine trees is a tricky slate stile over the wall. Cross over the wall and pick up the path which descends to the left on steeply sloping grass parallel with the wall. Go through gateway and follow path which at first goes left then right through a broadleaf woodland. Path becomes a more easily seen track as it goes down towards a fence. Go through the gate and turn left along a track. Go through the gate or over a stile to its right. The path through the wood now runs parallel with the river. Cross wooden stile and go on by a wet patch. The path climbs and at a T-junction turn right. The path leaves the wood through a gap in a wall and descends with the wall, right. There is an open section by the river side. The path then joins the track you came on, near the river bend. Follow it back to Grange.

A "Thwaite" in the Lake District is a clearing, a level, or a cultiv-
atable area in a wilderness. Stonethwaite is well named. It is a place
of stones. Scores of becks on the high fells of Grasmere, from Bowfell
and the steep sides of Glaramara pour into two becks; Greenup Gill
and Langstrath Beck; these converge into one, the Stonethwaite
Beck. When there are heavy storms on the fells Stonethwaite is
pounded by a raging torrent. Great stones are bounced along like
ping-pong balls. They jam and the beck changes course, tearing
away banks. Fields are scattered with stones which have had to be
painfully cleared regularly for generations. The run-off is so fast that
the beck is never the same. One moment it is gentle as a lamb; an
hour or so later it will be roaring like a lion.

This walk is therefore stony, in parts; and in others a little wet.
But it is otherwise a level and pleasant walk. Avoid it in wet weather.
Drive to Stonethwaite village. From Keswick this is seven miles up the
Borrowdale valley. Just after the village of Rosthwaite there is a
turning left (a minor road.) The sign reads "Borrowdale Church.
Stonethwaite. (Footpath only)", and a sign below reads "Unsuitable
for motor cars after Stonethwaite". Drive along this road until you
reach the village proper. After the first building on the left there is a
small open space. If you are unable to park here for other vehicles
return down the road by which you arrived and park on the wide
verge.

Just after this first building on the left a stone lane can be seen
leading off it to the left. It is signposted "Greenup Edge For Sargeant
Man, Langdale Pikes, Easedale Tarn & Grasmere." Take this and go
over the bridge, through the gate, turn right at the T junction and go
through another gate. The track passes through open woodland,
mainly ash. Those on the right, over the wall on the field side, have
been pollarded to provide winter feed for sheep. There is a group of
larch, then the view opens up just round the corner. Blocking the
valley head is the large bulk of Eagle Crag. No eagles dwell there
now; after many years of persecution there is little immediate chance
of their return. After another gate the way forks. The left-hand one
is the pleasanter way. Go through the gap in the broken wall and
continue. The fells on the right belong to Glaramara (2,560 feet).
The more immediate of its crags is Bull Crag. Go on by a group of
larch, and ford a stream. The way is now rather stony. Go between a
ruined barn and a sheep pen, and just after this there is a very old
misshapen yew tree on the left. Yew is the slowest growing of our
native trees. Its tough wood made the bows for the bowmen of
England.

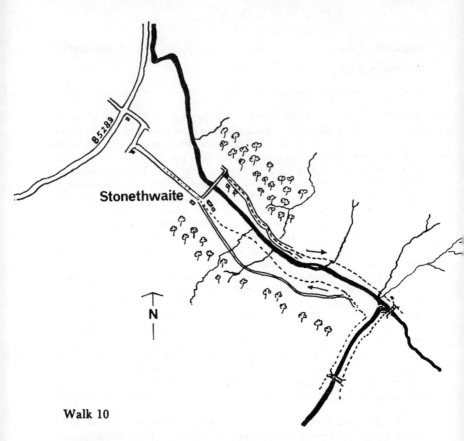

Stonethwaite

N

Walk 10

The path becomes green as it goes on between a wall right and a broken wall left. Go through a gate. The rushing beck is impressive hereabouts. It has scoured out a gully in the solid rock. At this point the path has been broken at the edge by flood. Uneasy walkers can avoid this short stretch by going up the little path to the left, but it has a steep descent back. The way is now over water-worn rocky ground. Ford another stream. The path gains a little height. If you were to continue right ahead you would cross Greenup Edge and reach Grasmere, six miles on. The path leading off up the valley partly obscured on the right, at the other side of Eagle Crag, goes by the Stake Pass to Langdale, also six miles on. When you come to some sheep pens, pass them on their left. Go alongside a fence, then turn its corner at the end and go over a stile. Then turn left and cross the footbridge. The local Highway Authority is quite good at replacing and repairing footbridges: in these valleys subject to floods it has to be. Go right on beyond, avoiding the wet land to the right.

A little further on there is rough wet ground to cross by stepping stones. To avoid the next wet section it is best to walk on the water-worn bedrock on the right. Continue on through a wall gap. Langstrath Beck is now on your right. After a quarter of a mile there is a group of birch trees on your right and then there is a small footbridge. Cross the bridge, closing the little wicket gate after you to prevent the sheep from crossing by it. Join the path and turn right. Just by the gate further on, there is a large oak with unusually large sideways growth caused by storm damage. Continue on down the gravelly path.

A little further on you will see a wall going down the right. Where this wall ends before the beck side there is a stile. Walk down and go through this. Walk alongside the beck on a narrow path, and along a green field. Cross the little beck by a slate bridge and then go up the bank under the trees to a stile in the wall ahead. Continue on following the beck side. If the walk is done in the holiday season there will be tents hereabouts and you need to take care over guy lines. A very rough stony section is crossed. Here a pretty beck used to go between stone walls but not long ago the stream became a boiling river and swept the walls flat. Go forward to a stile and gate. (If you use the gate close it after you.) Continue on on the same line over the next field to another gate followed by another. The next gate brings you on to a macadam road by the Langstrath Hotel. Your car is right ahead.

Watendlath is a pretty hamlet at the head of a valley running parallel to Borrowdale. It is situated by an equally pretty tarn, bridged at its outlet by a picture-book arch-bridge. Those who have read the novels by Sir Hugh Walpole will recognise the setting for "Rogue Herries" and "Judith Paris". Walpole enthusiasts make pilgrimages to the place. But it needs no literary associations to attract the tourists. It is a fine place . At one time (not so long ago at that) good walkers' guides recommended a walk up to Watendlath from Borrowdale road, by Ashness Woods and Surprise View (taken in on our walk number 7), then leaving the village to descend to Rosthwaite, and back along the road. In today's traffic the excursion would be frought with dire peril. It is no longer pleasant to walk up to Watendlath along the secondary road that leads to it from Borrowdale. On a busy day you could risk carbon monoxide poisoning apart from injuries! Nor indeed is it pleasant to drive to Watendlath. The road is narrow and there is a shortage of passing places. The last stretch is between walls, and their protruding stones bear evidence of many scrapes with colourful vehicles. Even though the National Trust, which owns this fine area, has put in a footpath for the last mile or so — muddy in places — the walk cannot be recommended. At the time of writing there is some talk about restricting traffic along this narrow road, so that it might be better enjoyed by walkers — there would then no doubt be a car park at the foot of the road. No one likes restrictions; but the only alternative would be to widen the road which would ruin the delicate beauty of the area.

Our walk is a straight up and down one from Rosthwaite along the ancient pack-horse route from that village. No apologies need be made. It is an excellent walk offering spectacular views. There is, however, a climb of over 800 feet, and time should be allowed for this. Allow two hours for the walk, adding a bit for age, heat, snow, idleness — and for refreshments at the hamlet.

Rosthwaite is five and a half miles from Keswick along the Borrowdale road. The path starts as a short stretch of macadam road going off left just before the village is entered. (Signposted.) There should be space on the verge to park here. Go up this short stretch of macadam road. A short way along it is a bridge over Stonethwaite Beck. The beck shines with multi-coloured stones. Just over the bridge turn left. (Signposted "Watendlath".) Go up the cobbly path. At the point where the footpath is subject to flooding, a higher walk level has been provided. Go through gate at the end of this and follow the footpath up to the right. Above this the path splits in

40

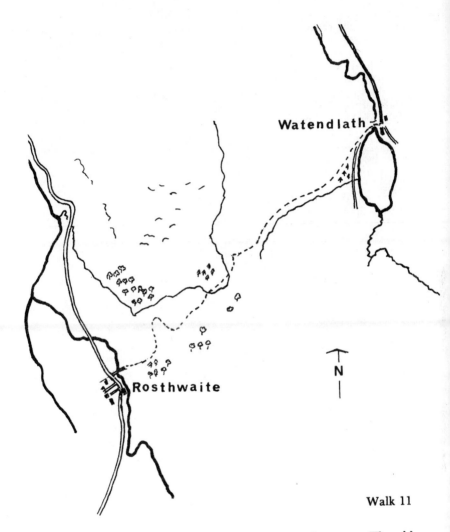

Watendlath

Rosthwaite

N

Walk 11

several places, impatient walkers having made short-cuts. The old winding way (if you can find it) is usually the easiest route. As you gain height there are good views into the head of Borrowdale.

Pass through a wall gap and go forward through trees over a slate bridge. The path roughens after this. There is a small wooded dell on the right with a little beck in it. As you get higher the path becomes .a green one, and there are telephone poles looking incongruous in this high wild setting. Looking back and to the left you can see the highest mountains in England. (You can view them better on the return journey, when you should be needing an excuse for a rest.) The first and nearest fell is Rosthwaite Fell at the end of the Glaramara range. Behind that is the huge buttress of Great End in the Scafells range. Its gullies long retain the winter snows and they are popular with climbers. Behind it, if the weather is clear, you should see a little point on the heavy lump of a summit. This is Scafell Pike, 3,206 feet and the highest point in England. To the right of this range, at the other side of the valley of Sty Head, is Great Gable, 2,949 feet, its right hand side chopped away into crags.

As the path summit is breasted, Watendlath Tarn appears òn the right below. On the descent the view is enhanced by the larch grove which frames it. The approach to the hamlet is made over the pretty arched bridge.

The return is by the same route as you came. Allow a good margin of time for the return as the steepness is not easy, and take care on the loose stones. The downward views can be enjoyed more easily. Do you see the great lump of Castle Crag in the middle of the Borrowdale valley on the right? Its ascent looks impossible—but it isn't, as we found on Walk 9! Behind it are the cruel-looking Eel Crags.

We are not sure who Johnny was, but his wood is listed as an area of "Special Scientific Interest" by the Nature Conservancy as it is a very typical example of an oak wood with an undercover of hazel, and it contains some very localised mosses and liverworts. Like most good things in the Borrowdale area it is in the care of the National Trust. This river-side walk, finishing on a low fell viewpoint, circles the wood. There are one or two wet patches, and footwear should be well treaded.

Park in Seatoller Car Park. This is right at the head of Borrowdale where the road turns to go over Honister Pass. Seatoller is the hamlet at the foot of the pass and the car park is just by the "Honister" sign. Leave the car park by the little wicket gate at the farm side of the car park. Turn right and you are presently walking with a wall right and a hedge left. The hedge is largely of birdcherry, and if you do the walk in May the blossom can be fine and fragrant. The birdcherry favours the highland areas of the north of Britain. Go through gate and continue on alongside wall. Shortly there is a fork, the right hand path is the less distinct of the two and this should be followed. Ford a little beck, avoid the wet patch beyond, and go through the iron gate on the right. Follow the path round left. This is the fringe of Johnny's Wood and there are some fine oak trees. Ash, birch and holly are also seen among the oaks which are "sessiles". This species, too, favours the highlands of Britain and though it can grow tall it does not generally attain the girth of the "pendunculate", the more common oak of lowlands. Notice that the moss grows so thickly on some of the trees that it supports the common polypody fern.

The path leaves the wood for a while by a broken wall, at the end of which bear left over the grass to pick up a grassy path. This goes parallel with a wall on the right. You move into the wood again. Go through gate. At this point some larches were once planted. There are two mountain ash. They are not well grown as they are suffering from lack of light. Mountain ash is the "magic tree". Pieces of it were once carried to ward off evil spirits and witches, or to counter the power of the "little people". At one time a beam of rowan (the other name for mountain ash) was put into a living room of a house to avoid its possession by witches and a block of the wood was built into ship's keels. Sometimes the wood was made into the shape of a cross. Of special value was the "flying rowan" which did not grow in the ground. This was very magical indeed and further on in the walk you will see some of this special wood. There is a peculiar birch "sculpture" on the right.

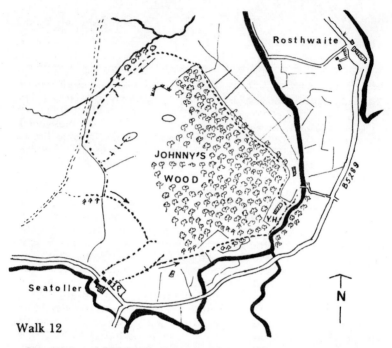

Walk 12

You are crowded between a crag and a wall. Go through wicket gate and the riverside is reached. You have to walk over some rough craggy land and along a crack in the rock. The river pools here are a beautiful green. You walk in front of the Longthwaite Youth Hostel. Before reaching the gate, however, at the far end of the property, turn left across the grass to the wall corner. Follow the wall round to the right.You pick up a path which goes behind a farm by two patches of wild iris. Just by the farm gate there is an elder-berry tree. These are trees often found near houses in these parts. At one time they were valued for their medicinal properties, a syrup made from the berries was taken warm for fevers and colds. Dried, the berries were used as a substitute for currants and medicinal tea was made from the flowers.

The path becomes a stone track. Hazel trees can be seen growing well about here. These usually grow in clumps as they send up many shoots after being cut. Hazel nuts were once a valuable Lake District crop, and tons of them went to market. The trees were, however, devasted by the charcoal burners in the last two centuries to feed the iron furnaces. The wood has always been valued for making baskets, shepherd crooks, walking sticks and broom handles. In summer here you may get a delicious scent from meadowsweet growing on the right. There are some more mountain ashes, growing crookedly in their search for light. The shamrock type plant growing on the woodland floor is wood sorrel. As this has a vinegar taste, its leaves used to be added sometimes to salads and "herb puddings". The way begins to climb a little. Go over stile or through adjoining gate. Still climbing, the path crosses a little beck. Shortly on the right is an ash tree which has accumulated so much leaf mould in its fork that a holly tree is growing in it. This is a wonder, but it is the rowan, growing similarly (or "flying") which is really magical. Search around this ash and you will find such a rowan in the fork farthest away! (In winter the rowan's shiny smooth bark contrasts with the rough grey bark of the ash it is growing on). Then again on the left just before you get to a large spreading oak a rowan is growing out of an alder clump. Just before the gate there is yet another of these magical trees, an even better example growing out of a hawthorn so vigorously that it appears to have split the trunk. Go through the gate and on the left you will see a silver birch growing out of an alder.

Continue up the path away from the wood. A grassy path leaves the stony one. You rise on towards the next wood. You reach a tree-clad gully. Follow the green path which curves away. This climbs, and when you pause for a breather, look back. You are looking over the Borrowdale valley. Across it is the tree-clad slopes of Grange Fell, and to its right you can see the path down to Rosthwaite from Watendlath. On the left, on your side of the valley, there is the rough steep hump of Castle Crag, scarred by old quarries. The path again follows the edge of the gully. You can hear a waterfall down to the right, but it can only be seen after leaf fall. A nearer approach down the steep is unsafe. The path levels off by a wall. As you reach the beck there is a wooden stile on the left, cross over this and go up a short section of steep bank opposite. Then the path bears right, forking shortly; keep to the right hand path which follows a more level way but becomes less distinct. Continue on — if you lose the path, roughly parallel with the wall you can see just to your right close on the other side of your valley. Presently there is a wall on the right by the beck-side. With your eye follow this up and you will see where it curves behind a knoll in front. Make for this point. The path should become more visible. The wall then on your right should be admired for the builder's craftsmanship. The stones fit perfectly together like a three-dimensional jig-saw puzzle. You can see the slightly rougher sections where repairs have been made to a lower standard. Most of the Lake District walls date from an enclosure movement begun towards the end of the 18th century. They still serve a useful purpose though nowadays it is difficult to find the labour to build and repair. That is why it is so tragic when they are damaged by thoughtless people. For instance if the "camstones" on the top of the wall, which lock it together and keep out the weather, are knocked off by accident and not replaced, the whole wall may begin to collapse around that point.

The path curves round with the wall and gives a view up to the head of Borrowdale. The jagged ridge of Glaramara is on the left, the hump of Seathwaite is in the middle, and to the right of that fell you see right up Grains Ghyll to the rough face of Great End on the end of the Scafell range—the roof of England. The energetic might like to climb the knoll on the left to get a better view. There is a faint path right up the ridge. From here you follow this right through some bracken to a broken wall. Follow this broken wall right to avoid a swamp just beyond it, then cross another broken wall and continue to climb up on to the rocky knoll. From here you have a fuller view of the Scafell range, and you can see Great Gable on its right. Looking the other way you can glimpse Derwentwater and Keswick beyond Castle Crag. Descend from this knoll the way you came up. Go back to the wall.

The path goes through a wall gap between the wall right and one coming in from the left. It goes through bracken to the right of, and below, a larch tree which is growing out of a crag. This is a place typically favoured for larch regeneration. The seedling cannot stand much competition but in such a craggy spot is is alone, its roots can take advantage of the clefts, and sheep cannot get at it sufficiently well to eat it. Keep to the left of the wet ground with care on slippery rock half-hidden in the bracken. You then make a steep descent to a stony track. The buildings of Seatoller can be seen below. There is a picturesque group of pines through the gate on the right, with a straight single larch. Turn left however to where the track forks at a gate. Go through the gate and on to a green track beyond which bend right, by four Scots pines. Descend through a gateway. Go through the gateway at the bottom, turn left through the village to the car park where you started.

The Keswick Stone Circle, usually known as the Castlerigg Circle, is reached by taking the Penrith road out of Keswick (not via the by-pass) and taking the first branch road to the right, signed 'Castlerigg Stone Circle'. At about one mile along this road, after passing a branch road to the right, there is the entrance to the site, marked by a National Trust sign. There is some parking space along the road side.

The Stone Circle is about three thousand years old, (give or take a year!) Such circles are sometimes called "Druid circles" but in fact they were in use long before the arrival of the Celts and their druids. Most assume that they were places of worship of some sort, and there is some evidence to suggest that they were also "calendars" so that the earliest settlers here could know when to sow and when to reap. Some experiments have been made in an attempt to prove the Circle's use in this respect. Unlike many circles there are no burials within the enclosure, which is slightly pear-shaped. There are 48 stones; there were probably more than this at one time. The setting, among the ring of hills, is impressive. This walk is from a pre-Christian place of worship, to the little Christian church of St. John's. It is a walk across fields surrounded by hills. It is marred by a few yards of bog, which can be avoided with patience and care; and a few yards of main road grass verge. If dogs are taken they will need to be on leash through the fields around the farms.

Having admired the stone circle, return to the entrance and into the lane again, and turn right. There are soon pine trees on the left and the lane bends. Just before the bend there is a gate on the right. Go through this on a faint path with the stone circle field fence on the right, and a wood on the left. The path goes into an open field; continue on, following the wall on your right. Presently a narrow stile will be seen in the wall ahead. Go on and through this. Walk forward and slightly left and a stile will be seen round the wall corner. Go over this, then aim to the right of the wood ahead to a stile in the wall corner. Walk alongside the wood, and at the end of it turn right to follow the hedge and then a wall. Follow the wall round and go through the gate. Close gate and go through the farmyard. Go along the road to the right of the house, then instead of going over the cattle grid go through the large gate to its left. Go forward keeping the old hedge on your right, then bend left towards the farm road. Go over cattle grid or through the gate alongside it and join main road with care. Go left on the grass verge for a few yards and then a stile in the roadside wall on the left is seen, with a signpost

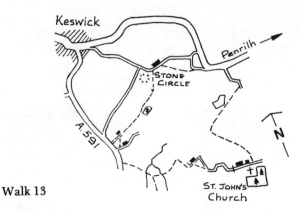

Walk 13

("Footpath to Church of St. John's in the Vale. 1 mile"). Go through
the stile and across the field bearing slightly right, then go through
the stile and down the stone ladder at the other side. The path is
clear then alongside a wall. There is a good view of Blencathra to the
left. The Helvellyn range is in front of you. The summit ahead on
this range is Great Dodd. The summit of Helvellyn is at the right
hand end of the range, hidden from view at this point.

Go through the gate at the bottom, then through the gate and over
the bridge. Immediately afterwards bear left and go towards the
corner of the field. This is a faint path leaving the more substantial
track. Avoid wandering from it, or walking two or more abreast
across this valuable grass crop. A white wicket-gate will be seen. Go
through it and across the bridge, then forward to a wooden ladder-
stile. Go over this and follow the fences round to the right. Cross
over the wooden ladder stile on the left and follow the track. Then
instead of following it when it bends left towards the farmyard, go
over the stone stile on the right. Leave the little sheep-pen
which may be beyond the stile and go forward over the rock
outcrops. A faint path will be seen, and over the rock it is worn
smooth. Make towards the right-hand side of the wall in front. A
stone stile can be seen beside an iron footpath sign. Cross the stile
onto a hard-surfaced track. Go across to the signpost ("St. John's in
the Vale Church") turn left up the track, and go along the zig-zags.

The track brings you to a gate and a kissing-gate with a plantation
on the right. Go through the kissing-gate and past the youth centre.
The tiny church of St. John's is just after this. It is only just over a
hundred years old, but it was built on the site of an earlier church.
Its setting is very pretty.

Opposite the church is a stone step-stile. Go over this. Go over the
little stream by bearing right, then go forward. The path is faint at
first. Way ahead a wall can be seen. The path goes to where the wall
dips through a hollow, and if you look at the objective and walk

48

towards it the path will then be seen. Blencathra is prominent on the right; Skiddaw ahead. Then here is the very wet ground. In fact one is reminded of the tragic end of the Lorna Doone story. The dastardly murder could have been committed in such a church, and the villain might have well gone to his sticky end under the trembling ooze at this point. You can avoid such a catastrophe by going well over to the left and making a very wide detour. If you can keep an eye on the objective of the dip in the wall you should not get lost. Keep to the right of the big crag. Bog can be distinguished from dry ground by the moss growing on the wet ground, and the lush green grass.

On reaching the wall you will find a stone step-stile. Go over it and through the hollow ahead. Below to the right is a tarn — Tewet Tarn. Make towards this. The way through the fence is just to the right of the wall. The large pike on the sky-line is Grisedale Pike. Eel Crag is to its left and before it is the rounded pike of Causey. Go along to the right of the tarn towards the gate in the wall. Go over the stile alongside it. Go on, bearing right. The walls to the left and right converge ahead. Head for this point and you will find a gate. Go through and down the field. (Close this important gate.) Follow the right-hand wall down to an awkward gate. Join the secondary road and turn left. If you do the walk in early summer you will enjoy the blue flowers of the native geranium — Cranesbill — with foxgloves and the blue climbing flower, vetch, all along the grass verge. This road joins a main road. Turn left and go along the very narrow grass verge which the highway authority have so generously provided for our safety. Keep children and dogs under strict bondage and be thankful that we have not far to go. At the bend in the road take the minor road signposted "Stone Circle". After this road crosses a bridge, go through the gate on the left. Go on to the next gate in the wall. Bear left and head for the next gate. Go through this. Our objective — the prominent farmhouse of Goosewell — is seen ahead. The right of way probably cannot be seen easily. Head for the farm and you will reach a small gate. Go through this on to the road and turn left. You are soon back at the stone circle.

If you dislike crowds this is probably as good a way as any to get away from them. It is a circular route from the village of Mungrisdale, going through a pass on the Blencathra (otherwise known as Saddleback) range. For a good way it follows the course of the river Glenderamackin. Glenderamackin? No, this book is not, for once, entering into the realm of fiction; that is the actual name of the river. Most place names in the Lake District are Norse, for the whole area was a Viking stronghold. There are, however, a few Celtic names left. Probably Blencathra is one. Helvellyn is almost certainly another. There are various theories about the origin of Glenderamackin. It sounds very Celtic; but those who favour Norse suggest that the "Glen" part comes from old Norse "Glenna"; a clearing in a forest. In Celtic a similar word means a narrow valley. But this is a long river eventually running into Derwentwater.

With tongue ever-so-slightly in cheek another suggestion could be added. To "glender" in Cumberland dialect means "to wander about in a dazed and aimless manner." Which could describe the movements of a river at its lower reaches; particularly this one just before it joins with St. John's Beck to become the river Greta. "A-mackin", also in Cumberland dialect means "a-making". This is also what a river does as it descends, picking up the water from the little becks as it goes. So this name could just be local dialect. Of course the more learned readers of this book will say this is pure nonsense. Anyway, let's not go "A-macking a song aboot it"; but let's go "glenderin aroond Sowter Fell."

We must add of course that Souther Fell is, or was, haunted. The story is a remarkable one. A whole spectre army has been seen marching across the shoulder of this fell. The phenomenon was first seen on Midsummer Eve in 1735. The observer, who first thought he was seeing locals coming from a market, was dismayed to watch a whole army coming round the fell. He could describe their movements in detail as he watched them for over an hour. Two years later on Midsummer Eve a local gentleman of standing, with his whole family, saw the same. At first under the impression that they were seeing the return of huntsmen, they then saw the great company appearing with their officers, mounted on horses, leading. They watched the monoeuvres for an hour between 8 pm . and 9 pm. Eight years later the ghostly army was seen by no less than 26 "respectable" people; and no doubt by a good many more who were less respectable. The 26 made an attested statement before a magistrate that they had watched the "vast number" of military for an hour.

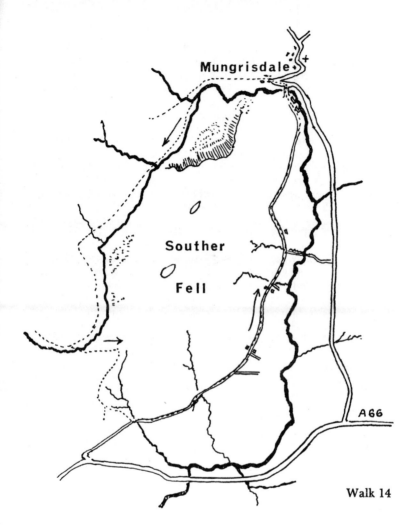

Walk 14

So if you wish to add interest to this walk — do it on Midsummer Eve!

The walk is not for a misty day. Good footwear is essential as there are wet sections. The beginning of the route is like wandering into a miniature Scottish highland glen. It follows an apparently ancient track. So well was the route of this path chosen that a climb is achieved with the minimum of effort. On emerging from the summit of the pass those with no heads for heights will worry for a short time perhaps, but the path is a safe one all the way. The last half of the walk goes gently along a quiet lane which is perhaps an example of how the Lake District roads must have looked in the days before the advent of the internal combustion engine. Flower spotters should carry their reference books for the second half of the walk too.

What better starting (and finishing) place than an inn? In fact, the Mill Inn at Mungrisdale. Take the Penrith road, A66, out of Keswick. The Mungrisdale road is on the left after seven miles, and the village is two miles up this minor road. Park without obstructing. The Mill Inn was once a mill. The river falls below it under an arched bridge making a green, cool, and artistic scene. Walk on from the bridge as if you were leaving the inn and the village. Almost immediately on the left is a lane, with a telephone box at the end of it. Walk up this lane past the farmyard and through the gates and onto the old track beyond. Ford a small stream. You are in a green valley surrounded by softly-shaped fells of Skiddaw slate. Ford another beck — if necessary go to the right to cross it at a narrower point.

Now don't follow the track to the right, but pick up a track which follows the river-side. The first part of this is very difficult to see as it crosses wet ground. This can be passed with care and a reasonably clear path is picked up beyond which gets clearer as you progress. The main vegetation here is bracken, but in June and July there are foxgloves, and a white carpet of bedstraw. Cotton grass blows in the wet areas. Muddy sections can be avoided by going higher to the right when necessary. Another beck is approached by stepping-stones. To cross it turn up right and there is a little plank bridge. A grassy path now rises gently. The next beck crosses the path and tumbles down a waterfall. A place to rest awhile if you need one for it is a pleasant little scene. If it is not possible to stride over this beck, take it below to avoid the wetness.

There is soon a bad wet section. If you must avoid it go below it for the water soaks through the stony ground. Another wet section beyond this can be avoided in a like manner. You have now reached some height, and if it were not for the water you can hear tumbling below you could hear a pin drop. Another wet section (all these wet sections would not be here if the path had been properly maintained over the years) is best avoided by going above it, fording a little beck which feeds the bog. Below by the river-side there are now trees, mainly mountain ash, which have grown here because the river sides are steep and the young trees could not be eaten by sheep. The river is neared again, and you will presently see a plank bridge below you. Your way lies across this, but you need not make a desperate descent to it. Follow the path right past it and you will see that the correct way zigs (or zags?) more gently towards it.

Cross the bridge and follow the path which climbs upwards to the left. On reaching the path summit look back at the way you have come and be proud of yourself! Directly behind you is the sharp outline of the Blencathra summit ridge. You should make out a spur coming off towards you which is aptly named "sharp edge". This is one of the routes up the mountain—not for complete novices. You are now, in fact, standing on the side of Blencathra.

Once over the summit you can look down into the green vales of Threlkeld Common. The fells on the skyline are those of Helvellyn. You are looking at the ridge end on, and the summit is obscured. Over to the right if there is clear visibility you might see the pointed summit of Bowfell, and to the right of this a gap, then Scafell Pike. These are well over fifteen miles away as the crow flies. After going over the summit go over to the right. The path is at first indistinct over wettish ground but as you go on it becomes quite clear as it takes the right hand side of the valley below. Take care over rough sections.

The path descends onto a grassy section. If you look back you will see again how well the old track makers chose their line for economy and ease of effort. Go through the gate, close it, and follow the indistinct path which goes parallel with the fence which is on the left. Go out through the gate onto the lane. Close gate. Turn left. Go through another gate. Now the plant spotters can get out their reference book. See if you can add to, and identify the list the author made on a June walk along here. Children will recognise the common omissions:

Germander speedwell; lesser and greater stitchwort; moss campion; bedstraw, foxglove, clover, golden saxifrage; wild rose—red and white; broom; lady's smock; barberry (in hedge—a wild rarity nowadays); forget-me-not; herb bennet; tormentil; spearmint; butterwort; brooklime. Tree spotters will note the pleasant grove of aspens.

After the first house, Souther Fell, the road has a cobbly surface almost all the way to the inn. Geologists will note the characteristics of the Skiddaw slate in the quarry holes.

"Vale" is an English word and rings rather strange in the Lake District where nearly all the place names are Norse or Celtic. The vale is noted for its enchanted castle—or was noted at one time. In the Lake District's "romantic" period when the area was newly-discovered by the aesthetes and intelligentsia, it was fashionable to go up the Vale of St. John's and imagine that you could see a beautiful castle at the end. One could mark out its gothic structure, with its towers and buttresses. Curiosity bringing the observer to a nearer position, he would see, to his surprise, that it was all an illusion. The buttresses and the towers dissolved into rock. The "castle" was just a rock. Indeed the rock is still marked as Castle Rock on the maps. The author is something of a romantic, and believes he also has imagination. But he has stared at that rock in all weathers; with his eyes screwed up; his head on one side; through the wrong end of a pair of binoculars, and cannot make a castle out of the rock at all. All that could be suggested was that in the old days the travellers were venturing into the largely unknown, filled with that strong Dutch courage for which the inns at that time were famous. However it is for you to test out your powers of imagination.

Park near Wanthwaite Bridge. To find this from Keswick take the Penrith road, the A66. After about 2½ miles watch for a road on the right signposted "Diocesan Youth Centre". This takes an old loop road, take the road from this, also signposted for the youth centre and after about a mile there is a wide left-hand bend with another narrow road leading from it on the right, signposted "St John's Church. Road unsuitable for cars beyond church". You should find a place to park just about here—on the grass verge at a pinch. To find the place from the Penrith direction turn off the A66 at Threlkeld down the B5322 signposted "Thirlmere, Windermere", take the first turning on the right after a little under a mile and a half, cross a bridge, and the point described above is just beyond it.

Having parked, walk up the road towards the church, but immediately on entering it turn left through the gate and onto the track. This goes alongside St. John's Beck and to Bridge House. Leave track at the house and walk on the grass by the river bank. There are some pleasant groves here, and throughout this valley trees make the scene. The beck curves around a beech grove. Go through the gate and here the path leaves the river bank and can be seen on the ground more clearly. Go on to gate. Castle Rock can now be seen ahead. Stare hard at it and make your own conclusions. It will be in view for quite a way on this walk.

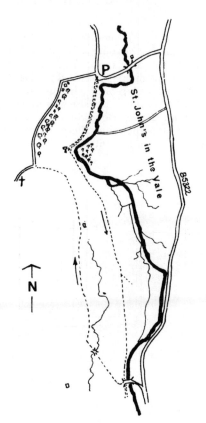

Walk 15

Continue walking on the same lines on less distinct path, and presently you are walking to the right of a fence past two birch trees. Go through the gate and forward. A ditch on the left is passed, then move over left-wards to a line of trees and a fence. Go over stile to the bank of the beck. Walk along the bank to the lovely arched bridge. This slender structure is a gem. The best view for photographers is beyond the bridge and looking back at it, with the hump of Blencathra as a background. (The right of way goes on along the bank beyond the bridge, over stile.) Take a last look at Castle Rock at this point for you are to turn back. Leave the bridge (Sosgill Bridge) right, go through the gate and bear sharp right across the field to a little footbridge, and beyond it to a kissing-gate. Turn right to follow the wall onto a path leading onto a **grassy track**. Go through gate.

The track climbs. There is a pretty waterfall up on the left. Go through another gate. On the shoulder of this path there is a good view from Blencathra ahead, to Castle Rock way over on the right.

55

There are some old sycamores soon around a ruin on the right. The old yew trees show that this was once a farmhouse as it was always the practice 100 years ago and more to plant a pair of yewtrees somewhere around a farmhouse. This is Rake How. Carry on to join hard road. St. John's church is on the left if you wish to visit it. It is not ancient, though it stands on the site of a much older church and the setting is very attractive. Go right to follow the road. There are some old oaks and beeches about here. Turn right to follow hard road surface to your starting-point.

Before plunging down the well-known waterfalls and into Ullswater, Aira Beck falls from its source in the north part of the Helvellyn range, down Deepdale and by Dowthwaitehead, a cluster of buildings at the top of a quiet valley. This walk goes to Dowthwaitehead, and returns via a section of the old coach road from Dockray to St. Johns.

Dockray is a village on the A5091 road which links Ullswater with Cumberland's Troutbeck, leaving the lake opposite Aira Point, three miles north of Glenridding, or six miles south of Pooley Bridge. From Keswick, the A5091 leaves the Penrith road after nine miles. On the north side of the bridge at Dockray (that is, the side farthest from the lake) there is a road leaving the village past the inn. Take this road and follow it to the top of the hill and the crossroads. Park here. There is a parking spot a few yards down the Dowthwaitehead road.

Walk down the road signposted "Dowthwaitehead". When the road forks you have a choice of routes. Both are pleasant. The left hand route is more adventurous as it crosses fields (wet in places). The right-hand route takes the road and is easier and drier. Both routes converge at Dowthwaitehead, and if those taking the road route think they have dodged all the wet they will be a little disappointed as the continuation takes them over some damp moorland.

First the left-hand route. Go down past the peculiar edifice belonging to Penrith RDC Waterworks. This strange castellated architecture is much favoured by water undertakings. Below there is a group of buildings. Just after the one on the right round its end and go through a gate. Go along the field side following a fence and then a wall. The rather broken wall curves left and there is a stone step-stile over the wall. Go over this stile. Just on the left at the other side in July there are the lush yellow flowers of monkey musk. Continue on in the same direction on an indistinct path. Presently you will see a gate in the wall in front; make for this. Now follow the wall down to the next gate. Keep close to the wall to avoid the boggy area, moving off left before you reach the corner. Go through the gate, turn right to the fence and follow this fence along. At the next gate there is a track, follow this through to the buildings at the end. Join the macadam road and turn right. On reaching the next building on the right as you turn the corner, there is a gate on the left. Go through this.

For the right-hand route simply follow the road down until you come to the hamlet at the bottom. On reaching the house on the left a wicket-gate will be seen opposite. Go through this.

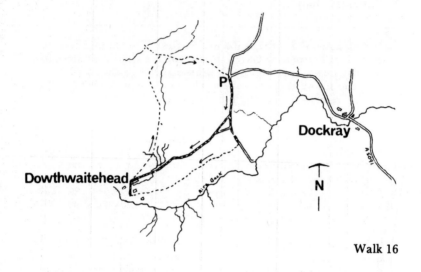

P

Dockray

Dowthwaitehead

N

Walk 16

Beyond the gate go through the wall gap and bear right. No obvious path is visible at first. But as you climb up there will be seen a pleasant green path in front of you, old and well made. There is a grotesque larch tree on the right. As you climb the view over the valley is most pleasing. When the path forks, do not take the one on the right, but continue climbing left. Ford a little beck. Zig-zag left on a rough section, and go off right up a steep grassy path towards a little gate you can see in the wall on the sky-line. Go through this gate, pick up a path which zig-zags left and follows a wall to a corner. Go straight ahead at this corner on the same line, when this grass path bears right however go down hill to the left. Make for the small grassy mound in front. Go over it and then continue on the same line beyond it keeping the little beck just to your left. Then on the same line, cross the beck at a convenient point and make towards a gate which you will see at the end of a wall opposite. Just before you reach this you will be on a hard road. This is the old coach road from St. Johns to Dockray. Turn right and go along it to the wicket gate at the end, and you are back at the crossroads where you started.

High above Thirlmere at its northern end are the earthworks of an ancient hill fort. These pre-Roman British strongholds were primitive affairs making the best use of natural features. Earth walls were thrown up, and by the same action a deep ditch was left. Over the centuries, Nature has hidden the scars fairly effectively. The works of this fort can be made out but it is difficult to imagine it as it must have been.

Forts are hard of access. This naturally means that the walk to it is somewhat steep. Strong footwear is a "must". Nearly all the walk is through forest and anti-midge preparations are recommended for summer walking! The way to the fort is a public footpath. From it the route is by a forest road with no legal right of way. However, you may walk it by courtesy of Manchester Corporation, which owns the forest, provided that you guard against risk of fire, close gates, and leave no litter of any kind. The return journey downhill is easy and pleasant.

Park your car at the open area at the road junction on the west side of Thirlmere dam. To reach this from Keswick take the A591 Windermere road. After about five miles prepare to turn right at the end of the dual carriageway, taking care as this is a fast road. Turn right down the secondary road. This goes over the dam and the parking spot is just at the other side at a road-junction. Coming from the Threlkeld direction via St. John's in the Vale, turn right on reaching the major road, and the turning is first on the left. From the south it is the first turning after the St. John's junction.

Leaving the car, facing the same way as you arrived, take the road to the right. Very soon on the left you will see two sandstone gateposts. The path starts just short of these gateposts and goes up through the trees. Douglas firs. A track, gouged out by timber extraction, is joined. Follow it leftwards. Rough parts of the track can be avoided by diverting right a little. At fork continue upwards; this is just after a bridge. There are two paths going upwards. The one on the left has been spoiled by timber extraction so take the one on the right. This forks, but do not be tempted off the ascent. Keep climbing. A reasonable track should soon be joined. In soft ground about here you may see the tracks of red deer. The fierce looking crag seen on the left through the larches is Raven Crag, very popular with rock climbers. At the point where the track is obscured by a landslip keep climbing and head left a little and a path will soon be joined, more rough but most easily seen.

At the path-top a forest road is joined. Walk on down the road

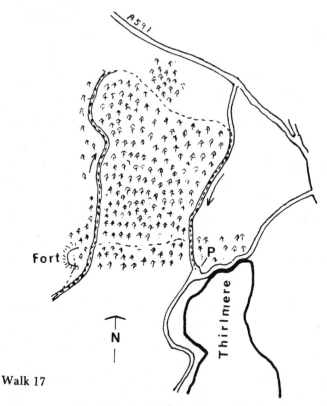

Fort

Thirlmere

N

Walk 17

until you come to a point where it has been widened out to allow timber loading and turning. At this spot turn right into the bay and head right, on a course almost parallel to the road along which you have just come. Head through the trees without losing height. This route might seem rather roundabout but it is to avoid deep swamp! A faint path should be seen. You go through birch trees with a heather-covered knoll in front of you. Cross the first ditch of the earthworks then climb over the first mound and, following the same course, go down into the next ditch, then climb up the crag by the faint path working up to the right and zig-zagging left. To reach the highest point go over to the right following the earthwork up. A short steep section goes under a mountain ash, and a faint path goes up and round to the left. The summit is then easily reached through the bracken and bilberries.

You can see right down the valley to the vale of St. John's. Skiddaw is prominent on the left, and the mountain on its right is, of

course, Blencathra or Saddleback. The fierce crag across the valley is
Iron Keld. Note how the beck opposite has cut a great groove into
the fell side. After a rest on this pleasant perch, return from the
summit by the route you came up. Go back to the forest road by the
same route too. (Short cuts through the mud can be very unpleasant.
Was this one of the fort's defences?) On joining the forest road turn
left. Walk back along the road the same route but this time walk
past the footpath by which you arrived, and go on along the forest
road.

This is a pleasant way through spruce and pines, passing round an
impressive crag face. When another road comes in from the
left carry straight on. At the bottom, note how the grass can grow
under the deciduous larch trees, allowing controlled grazing by
sheep; the cover of evergreens does not allow grass growth. At the
bottom of this road another one comes in from the left. Go right.
Go through gate to T-junction and turn right. The crag opposite
now is Castle Crag. There is no castle on it, nor was there ever. It
is another rock-climbers' crag. Go through another gate and go onto
a road. Turn right. This road eventually brings you to the starting
point. It is a quiet road but it is as well to keep a good look-out
for vehicles.

Before Manchester Corporation dammed Thirlmere, virtually destroying the hamlet of Wythburn, an important track left this settlement, going over the Armboth Fells to Watendlath and Borrowdale. The track is still there, though almost lost in mire on the summits. The fell has the reputation of being the wettest in the Lake District; Manchester chose well for its water supply. However, the first part of this track, as far as Harrop Tarn, makes a very pleasant walk. Everyone can do it, though its steepness will slow down the less energetic and some wetness cannot be avoided. There is a headless ghost at the tarn, it is said, but this is a minor hazard hardly likely to be met in daylight.

Thirlmere is reached by the A591 from Keswick — the Windermere road, turning right at the end of the dual carriageway to go along Thirlmere's western shore road. From the bottom (dam) end of the lake go abut 3¾ miles. The road cuts through a rock, on the left there is a little gateway with steps up a rock beyond it. (If you can park here for a moment, there is a good view from this rock, over Thirlmere to Helvellyn's slopes). Shortly after this there is a big gate on the right. There are two more cuttings and shortly after this there is a loop lay-by on the right between pine and beech trees. Park here.

Leave the lay-by and walk on in the same direction in which you arrived. After the road crosses a beck there is a distinctive smooth crag up upon the right. After passing this crag turn a corner and there is a gate on the right with a signpost. Go over stile, walk towards and to the left of the crag. Avoid the wetness by going towards the crag. The crag is a good viewpoint. After it go forward and upwards towards rough ground and juniper bushes ahead, skirting the wet ground as best you can.

The great fell across the lake, of course, is Helvellyn. Manchester Corporation's tree planting has sketched hard lines on its flank but under new and enlightened forestry policy these will be a thing of the past. The mountain's summit is out of sight. The main path from Wythburn can be seen going up the hollow.

Follow the path you are on, however, as it zig-zags parallel with the beck you should be hearing on your right. One or two cairns mark the route, though they are rather unnecessary. Flower spotters will note the insect-eating butterwort, and the little yellow flowers of tormentil, in the wetness about the rocks. The path follows a fence, and then the path crosses the fence by an eccentric stile and goes into the wood among pines and Norway spruce. A muddy section is

62

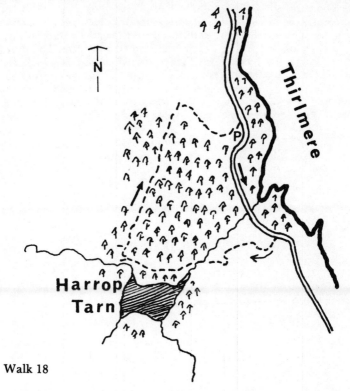

Walk 18

crossed by a cat-walk. The path reaches a beck which must be crossed to follow the path on the other side. Harrop Tarn appears on the left. At the best viewpoint Manchester Corporation have provided rude wooden seats. There are yellow water lillies on the tarn. Luckily these are out of public reach or they would have disappeared, some folk being like they are. (Water lillies look all right, but usually smell abominably anyway!) The setting of the tarn is pretty, and the planting enhances rather than spoils the tarn. The Corporation planted beeches hereabouts. Many of them have suffered from red-deer damage. There are still red and roe deer in the wood — but they are not as plentiful as they are in the forests in the southern Lake District.

The path rises with a beck on the left, and then there is a Y-junction. The right-hand way is a hard forest road. Take this. It leaves the beck and is joined by another track from the left, shortly. Continue on. Another track joins from the left and then a descent is begun. There is an old alder swamp on the right. Helvellyn can again be seen over the tree canopy ahead. In one of its gullies you can see an old mine, which began well but became unprofitable.

Presently the wood is left, and a breathtaking view opens up. From this angle Thirlmere looms natural and not at all like a reservoir. Go through awkward stile; a high one. Immediately afterwards turn right to follow the fence down. There should be a good display of foxgloves in season at this point. The path zig-zags away from the fence. Go through gateway and the path curves left away from the fence and towards the group of pine trees. Join the road by the gate. Close it, and the lay-by car park is just on the right.

Lowther Castle

Aira Force

Castlerigg
Stone Circle

Packhorse Bridge
over the Pasture
Beck, Hartsop

The geology of an area determines its landscape. The Lake District
has such a varied landscape because of its extraordinary geology — so
much variety in so little a space. The rocks of the Borrowdale
volcanic series provide the dramatic craggy landscape; the ancient
rocks which constitute the Skiddaw slate series make up the smooth-
lined bulk of the Northern fells, and of Black Combe in the south-
west. Looking northwards from Hallin Fell (Walk 23) there is a
different form of landscape of gentler hills and fertile plains, a
landscape of Old Red Sandstone and limestone. In it are the ancient
seats of Dacre and Dalemain. To walk here is like being in a different
country. Indeed this is the border county with its turbulent history.

The walk goes by Dacre Castle, Dacre's ancient church, and by
Dalemain Park. There are no hills of any height to climb, but
some of the walk is by grass paths, and by the riverside, so waterproof footwear is desirable. The walk starts at the car park at the
foot of Ullswater, at Pooley Bridge, on the west side of the bridge.

The way is by the path which you can see on the west side of the
car park along the edge of the wood. At the time of writing access to
it is through the entrance to the car park and over a stile. Follow this
path through very mixed woodland. The path rises into oaks. When
the path eventually comes close to a fence as it curves left round
the wood, a stile will be seen over the fence. Cross this. Go forward
and left towards a gate in the fence and hedge opposite.
This leads onto another path alongside a fence going off to the right.
Walk along this fence to a gate at its far end. Turn left through
this gate and head for the gate opposite. You reach a road. Opposite
you will see two gates, one on either side of a sycamore tree. Go
through the one on the right. Follow the fence. Go through gate and
continue with fence. There are some old oaks at the end of this path
before it reaches a gate. There is also quite an old sycamore on the
right of the gate. You join a macadam lane, and here turn right. Go
on to a T-junction and turn left. Walk along the grass verge, and you
lose height towards the village of Dacre. The castle can be seen on
the hillside opposite.

Go over the arch bridge across the river (Dacre Beck). You will
see that the river slides over a sandstone bed and perhaps observe the
bridge itself is built of the same material. Continue on up the road,
and on the side of the barn on the right you will see that it is
built from a mixture of sandstone and limestone, and the roof is of
sandstone. A road joins from the left but continue on into the pretty
village, and take the turning on the right to the church. The church

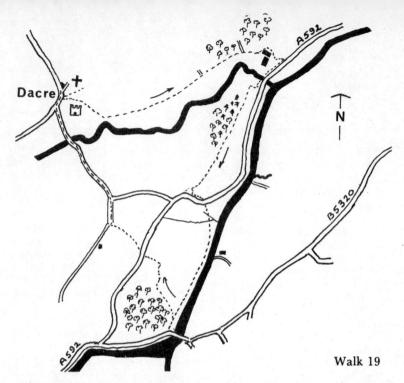

Dacre

N

Walk 19

stands on the site of the Saxon monastery mentioned by the Venerable Bede in his history. All that remains are a few traces of foundations, and an old drain. The present structure dates from Norman times. The round piers are dated around 1250, the octagonals show some reconstruction around 1400. There are some stone fragments of interest (a leaflet giving information about the church is available). On the south side of the chancel is a stone traditionally said to represent the "peace of Dacre" signed in the year 926 between Athalston of England and Constantine of Scotland.

In the churchyard are four mysterious stones of unknown origin but they probably came from the Castle. Going anti-clockwise from the north west the first depicts a bear asleep with his head on a pillar. The second, a bear is attacked by a cat. The third bear tries to shake the cat off. The fourth bear eats the cat. Maybe there is a moral to the story? It is a stern warning to cats anyway.

Dacre is named after the family of Dacre. One of the early members of the noble family served at the siege of Acre, in the Holy Land (hence d'Acre). Walk back a little way into the village and before you reach the junction there is a small green. Opposite it, on your left, is a gate with a stile alongside it. Go over the stile and along the track which goes by Dacre Castle. The castle is a residence and is not open to the public but the right of way passes under its walls. The castle was built in 1350 and has had fortunes which varied with

66

that of the Dacre family. Most famous, or infamous, of the Dacres was Leonard, who led a rebellion against Elizabeth the First, probably dictated by self-interest as he gained land by it; but he was defeated close by the river Golt in 1569 by forces under Lord Hunsdon, Elizabeth's cousin. The castle was restored under the ownership of the Earl of Sussex in 1675, and there was further restoration about 1789.

Just after the castle the track forks. Take the left-hand one. Walk alongside a plantation and at an old gateway the track curves off to the left. Go through gateway, continue on along an almost flat, straight track. Go through gate. Alongside the track is a line of trees; a planting of poplar and oak alternatively. Notice how the fast-growing poplars have outstripped the slower-growing hard-timbered oak. Go through another gate. There is a hedge on the left and according to an old practice, some of the trees have been allowed to grow on, but some horse-chestnuts and pines have also been put in. A farm drive joins from the left, continue onward. Go through a gate. There is a wood on the left with some tall trees including beech and elm. A track joins from the left, continue on. There is a high wall on the right as we approach the hall of Dalemain.

Enter the yard, then go through the archway on the left. Just along here if you look left you may be lucky enough to see fallow deer, for this is the hall's deer park (not open to the public). Fallows are not a native deer like the red and the roe, which are both wild in the Lake District. Fallows were introduced and in some areas of Britain, notably the New Forest, they have become wild. Hereabouts they are park deer, somewhere in size mid-way between the roe and the red. They are dappled. In roe and red only the fawns are spotted.

Go forward across the cattle-grid, and follow the hard-surfaced road round. This macadam road forks — turn left to join main road. Turn right and walk with care. On the right is the large front of Dalemain, seat of the Laytons at one time, and now of the Hasells. The road crosses a bridge. Look on the right. Ignore the first gate on the right after the bridge. Watch for the next gate. Go through this gate and go on across the field at an angle to the left towards the edge of the wood. The path is difficult to see but can be picked up at the wood boundary. Go on, keeping the wood on your right, and go through a gate. Forward of this the path is better defined. At the corner of the wood continue on (ignoring the gate on the right) go through the gate in front and continue alongside a fence. Go through another gate and follow fence. The path is again indistinct but follow the fence round. A wall is reached with a blocked stile. Turn left here and go down to the gate. Join the road and turn left. In a few yards, on the right, there is a gate. Go through this. Continue on at a leftward angle on an indistinct path towards the river. A path is picked up on the river bank which goes by a series of stiles and eventually brings you out at the car park where you started.

This walk leads from Aira Force, Ullswater's well-known waterfall (two and a half miles north of Glenridding) and goes through old park land with good views, returning at a lower level.

Park in Aira Green car park. Leave by the kissing-gate at the far end of the car park as you are going to the falls. Go across the field. Join the track at the far end of the field, following it through the kissing-gate on the right into the Aira Force wood. Cross the footbridge, bearing round right, on well defined path. Through another kissing-gate and over a wooden footbridge. Then up the steps to the right. Go up the path to a higher level. You pass a cedar tree and a magnificent Sitka spruce. Path undulates by the river side. Take the left fork to stand on the pretty stone bridge which is a good viewpoint though the far side of the bridge is a better one. Rejoin the path and take the left fork up the stone steps. Go up to the right, then left up some more steps. Continue on the better path. Turn left onto the bridge which gives a good view down the falls.

Do not cross the bridge but go back onto the path and continue climbing. Go forward on a green footpath. Very shortly the path reaches a T-junction with another green footpath. Turn right and continue down it until you meet a path turning left at the bottom. Follow this path which runs parallel to a fence then take the fork left and climb up the hill side. This is fairly steep but is not too far. When you reach the top of the first rise there is a big boulder. Stop here and admire the view. Looking right back the way you have come the first fell is Sheffield Pike, behind that is the summit of Raise where the skiers find sport in winter. Helvellyn is behind and to the left of Sheffield Pike. In the foreground to the left is Birkhouse Moor. The fell across the lake is Place Fell, and there is a beautiful view of the higher reaches of the lake.

Continue on. The incline below is steep. Children should be warned not to throw or roll stones, there being no telling where they might end. Keep on following the path, ignore the sheep trods which leave it. The true track is the better defined one. The higher the climb the wider the view; stop often and enjoy it. The beautiful airy path turns left slightly round a corner, and there is a crag on the right with a cairn on it, an excellent viewpoint, right down the middle section of the lake. The path which we want to reach eventually is directly below this crag, and there is a path to it; but this is a path used by climbers and cannot be generally recommended. Retrace your steps, from the cairn, and follow the

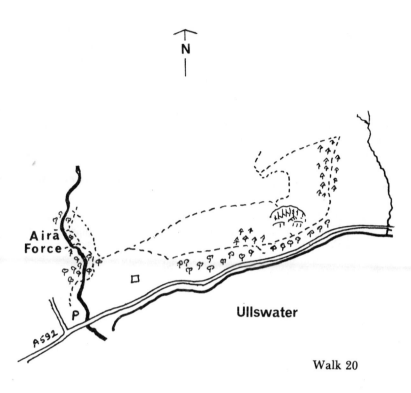

footpath on uphill. The path continues very attractively, with good views down the lake. Opposite can be seen the beacon on Hallin Fell and the High Street range is behind. The path goes right round the corner and you find you are walking with your back towards the lake. Continue on until you go so far round a corner that you seem to be doubling back on yourself. Then the footpath goes round to the right and starts to climb. But down to the right there is a tongue of land, standing higher between two hollows. This is where you should turn and descend. (The author made a cairn here which might still be visible.)

The descent is rather steep at first. Take it slowly, keeping to the right to avoid dampness. The line of an old broken wall is crossed. Go down towards the little beck with the alder trees. Choose the easiest way down. Keep to the right of the beck and go alongside the plantation. At the far side of the plantation turn right to follow its bottom edge. The lake will come into view again. Walk just inside the wood to avoid the wet sections. The trees are Sitka spruce and pines. As you proceed the planting is of larch. Look out for the red squirrels.

Soon, as you go along the edge of the wood, a path becomes apparent, striking into the wood a little way. This continues on a contour, the wood falling off to the left. You now leave the wood, crossing over a broken wall under a crag face. For a way the path is fairly rough, and needs care. It rises a little over loose stones, then goes along more easily on grass. A large old ash tree is reached just to side of the path. The crags above may have climbers on them; it is a practice area for the Outward Bound School. Continue on path which is more or less on the level, ignoring a path zig-zagging up, right. There is an old hollow ash tree with a big boulder alongside it with a cairn crowning it. Continue on, on built up path. This is quiet, clear and easy. There is a grotesque looking tree below to the left, a monster hollow oak. Then there is a monster ash tree on the right with a rough seat below it. The path runs alongside a large plantation.

Another path joins from the left. Our path progresses between a plantation right and an alder swamp on the left. The plantation is left and the built-up path continues through the alders. An open area is reached, and the path goes alongside a fence. The building left goes under the strange name of Lyulph's Tower. There is another tree curiosity nearby. A large ash tree is growing from between two boulders and appears to be forcing them apart, and flowing all over them. At path junction turn left into the Aira Force woodland again, rejoining the path by which we left.

Waterfalls should ideally be admired after heavy rain. This walk takes us from one impressive waterfall to another — but care should be exercised over wet, smooth rocks.

Park in Aira Green car park. Leave by the kissing-gate at the far end of the car park, and follow the path across the field, through the kissing-gate into the wood, over the footbridges then up the higher path and left. The first view is from the little stone bridge. Rejoin the path and continue up to the second bridge. This is the downward view of the big fall. Do not cross the bridge, continue up the side of the beck by the path on its right. The beck tumbles over steps, and

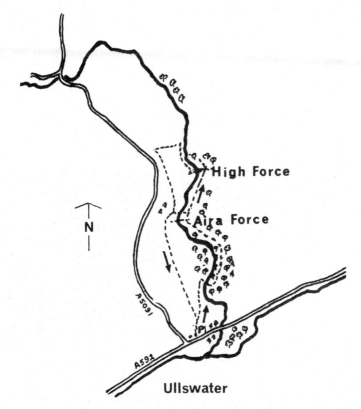

slides over hard smooth rock, and seeks out little spouts. The path is rather wet. Watch for dippers—the little shy dark bird with the white front and the short tail, which can dive under the water for food. In places the beck has cut its way under the bank to produce little caves and there are potholes cut into the bed by swirling pebbles. Take care of children in the party where the path rises to some height over the beck. At one point the path leaves a precipitous section to go up the hillside behind an oak tree. A better defined path is joined at a T-junction. Turn left. At the fork, turn left and cross the footbridge.

At this point the beck speeds through a narrow gorge and quite a way below. At the other side of the bridge turn right but take care if you go near the edge as it is slippery. Just a little further on is where the beck speeds along a flat section before dropping into the gorge. Go up the path. Where you are "crowded" between the beck and the wall go close to the wall, keeping to higher ground. You then reach another waterfall known as High Force. From the beck side it can be admired, though the main force is obscured by a rock doorway. You can see the force from a rocky promontory above this. But do not get too close as the rock is mossy and slippery. Above the falls the water slips over a hard rock pavement. Linger here by all means, but just above this is the step-stile through the wall on the left. This is the route. Go across the field along a faint path opposite, towards a gate and stile in the far wall. Go through neither, but follow the wall down on the field side of it. Soon several paths are seen. Take any of them down and well below a plantation. A little wicket gate is reached, just above the falls again. Go through it and turn right. Go up the wooden steps and round to the left. Do not go down to the beck but continue on to a kissing-gate and into a field. Go forward on grassy path, past the old ash trees, and bear left on a faint path, over a wooden step stile, and down to the car park kissing-gate.

There are several walks in the National Park which *must* be done because they typify the unique beauty of the Lake District. One is the walk from Howtown, along the lake side to Patterdale. The views almost all the way are excellent, and there are rocky bays to linger by, and grassy glades to picnic in. The walk offers no difficulty to anyone unless one counts the short stretch of busy footpath-less road at the end.

All the walks in this book begin and end at the car. This one is rather different as it is preceded by a trip on the lake "steamer". You should park your car in Glenridding, at the head of Ullswater, and board the motor-yacht at the public pier. The Ullswater Navigation Company run a regular service on the lake. At the time of writing this the morning boat for Howtown leaves at 11.30, arriving in Howtown at noon. Taking a packed lunch (and an emergency ration of chocolate) you could be back at your car at tea-time, after seeing some superb scenery.

Howtown is the boat's first call. Disembark, leave the pier, and turn right, cross the footbridge and continue to follow the lake shore. A wall and a fence are crossed by stiles. Continue to follow the lake shore by the track. At the gate go through stile and go left up the hillside (signposted). Go through the wicket gate at the top and turn right. Although you have left the lake at this stage you are compensated by excellent views right. The path rejoins the lake-side down a steep way through an oak wood, and the shore-line is broken by rocks. You pass through a lovely broad-leafed wood largely of beeches, oaks and elms. The elms are "wych-elms". The common elm is a rarity in the Lake District. One awkward point on the path is a slippery rock, but there are several choices of routes up or around this. A worse point further on has been made safe by the National Park's warden service. Two walls are crossed by stiles and you walk along the shore side of a meadow.

The path bends left to go through a gate, then go slightly left again to go through the next gate, and on to a stile alongside another. There is a track joined here, look left at the magnificent sycamore tree here. You pass under larch trees, there is a fine farm-house to attract artists on the right. Cross the bridge, pass through gate, and turn left along macadam road, and just after the cottages, turn right again to follow footpath—a broad one alongside a wall all the way. After a beck is crossed the path becomes a green one, and at the next bridge cross a bridge to follow the wall up.(There is a water-fall up the fell-to the left.) There is a steep section and then when the wall corner is reached at the top the path forks. Take the one falling

73

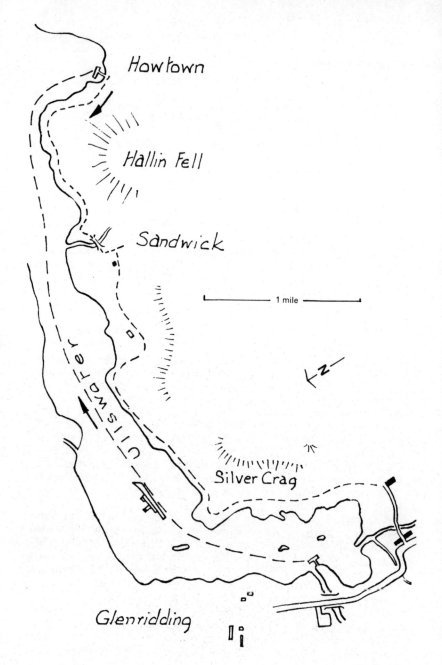

Howtown

Hallin Fell

Sandwick

1 mile

N

Silver Crag

Ullswater

Glenridding

Walk 22

to the right. This path is delightful, with good views of the lake again. The path now begins to climb as the surroundings become craggy. The heights above, which seem to lean over towards you, are clothed with dark green junipers broken up by graceful silver birch. At the highest point on the path there is a grassy viewpoint offering a pleasant resting place.

The path descends through woods of silver birch, at their best in autumn colours. The woods end in an open area and there is another fork. Continue down the right hand one, parallel with the lake shore. A bay is reached and the path rises again to the upper corner of a conifer wood. A wall is followed and the path becomes a track. Where this is joined by another track from the left look for the unusual oak tree on the right. This is an uncommon "Turkey Oak" with deeply jagged leaves. The track goes through a gate into a farm yard. Turn right between the buildings to follow the track towards the village of Patterdale.

On joining the main road turn right. Now follows a short dangerous section here on the bend where there is no footpath. There is a quiet pleasant walk then, on footpaths which end by a gateway on the left. Make your way over to the lake shore when safe to do so. The footpath proper starts at the boat landing again and you are soon in Glenridding.

Hallin Fell summit offers one of the National Park's greatest views. One can look over Ullswater, and on very clear days away north into Scotland. It stands beside the high entrance into the unspoilt valley of Martindale with its ancient and very simple little chapel. The walk described visits the viewpoint and the chapel. As it is a figure-of-eight walk with the car in the middle, it can be divided into two short walks. The only snag to this splendid round is the approach road. The road from Pooley Bridge down the east side of Ullswater is very narrow. On busy days in the season it takes traffic from the local camp and caravan sites, and more to the Howtown public landing and steamer pier. As road "improvements" would ruin this side of the lake delays at peak times have to be tolerated. The best advice that can be given is to do this walk on a mid-weekday or a non-bank-holiday. It is largely a walk on grass, and smooth-soled footwear could be dangerous.

From the hamlet of Pooley Bridge take the Penrith road for a short distance, then take the first turning right, and the first turning right again for Howtown. Howtown is reached after four miles along this narrow road. It is not a town by any stretch of the imagination and when you reach the cattle grid you have passed it. Go on up the very steep hill with hairpins — first gear may be required. Go right to the top of the hill and you will find room to park near the church.

The path starts up the grassy slope opposite the drive to the church. Go upwards to the wall and follow it, right. At the path fork continue left to follow the wall up steep grass. At the wall corner continue on. There is a pile of stones on the right with a fork, right. Continue on upwards on the broad grassy track. Pausing for breath and looking left you see the two valleys; Martindale on the left leading upwards to Bannerdale and the deer forest, and Boredale on the right. They were both scooped out from Place Fell by glaciers in the ice age. Red deer might be seen with binoculars, particularly in winter. There are also half-wild fell ponies in the area. Notice how the valley-bottoms are green and lush in contrast to the bracken and heather-covered slopes around. Take your time and you will eventually approach the summit, the wide grassy track narrowing a little. Ahead there is a little hause. A hause, be it explained, is the Lake District name for a saddle, or a pass, or a depression in a hill summit. (The motor road you climbed up by the hairpins is locally known as "Martindale Hause" as it is a pass through the hills into the dale). Beyond this little hause is a grassy platform. Cross it bearing right and climb a little and you will see a stone cairn,

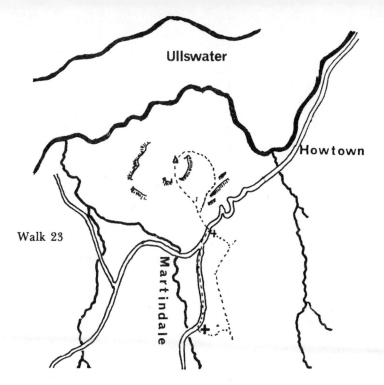

Ullswater

Howtown

Walk 23

Martindale

square-shaped, on the summit. As you reach it the views burst upon you — a dramatic revelation missing only the sound of a heavenly choir or a fanfare of trumpets.

Across the lake, way over on the left, you see the Helvellyn range, with the pointed peak of Catstye Cam which was once thought to be higher than Helvellyn, but is 101 feet short of Helvellyn's 3,118. Prominent on the right of the long Helvellyn ridge are the mountains of Blencathra, and beyond it Skiddaw which overlooks Keswick. You can wander about this open summit to pick up various viewpoints. For instance, if you walk back to the grass platform near the hause again, but this time turn right to descend by a natural hollow, you will presently come to an edge with an airy view down to the lake over the little hamlet of Sandwick. Retrace your steps to the summit cairn. With your back to the lake and looking east and south there is the long ridge of High Street. "Street" suggests a Roman road. In fact, a Roman road ran right along the summit ridge, largely following an ancient British road. Why along such a high ridge? In ancient times the whole of the valleys were covered in dense forest, scrub and swamp inhabited by the wild red deer which still roam the area, as they did long before man came upon the scene at all. It was much easier to walk, or ride, along this straight ridge once the road was made.

To descend, leave the cairn north-eastwards towards the foot of the lake (Pooley Bridge). Follow the grassy path which divides temporarily into two (going in the same direction). A cairn which is another viewpoint appears on the left. Continue on the grassy path taking care on the steepness. The path levels off and curves right. Continuing on, there is a level with a steep slope, left, to the lake. A path joins from the left by a wet area which might become a small tarn after rain. Continue on and there is a cairn on a little hill in front. The now broad green path goes to the right of this but a diversion to the cairn is worthwhile. From the cairn, walk towards the lake along the little ridge, then right the few yards to the next cairn, which offers views down towards Howtown and the steamer pier. Turn sharp right to follow the path back towards the wide grassy path you just left. Continue left, down it, when you rejoin. The church appears below and the path steepens. Turn right by a cairn, and at the fork turn right on the easier route. You rejoin the path by which you ascended, at the wall corner. Descend by the wall to the starting point.

Walk past the church gate and follow the wall on the right to pick up a track by a little tarn. Go to the right of the tarn still following the wall. Follow the wall right round the corner past (not through) the gate, and on. (The path above on the fell side cuts the corner but the way is rather rough). At the top of the hill follow the path by the wall side again. As you go forward Martindale is seen below you with its pretty arch bridge and its chapel, looking from this angle like an old barn, partly obscured by a crag. The narrow path moves away from the wall as it cuts a corner. The wall side is joined again further on. Now follow the wall round and down towards the little chapel, picking up the path which zig-zags down to avoid the steepness.

The interior of the church is starkly simple and for that reason strangely moving. This is the place where simple people worshipped and there are no elaborate memorials and stone effigies of knights. The existing walls were built in 1633 but they were built on foundations that already existed and there has been a chapel here for many centuries. The old square holy-water stoup is reckoned to be 14th century. On it are the marks of arrow-sharpening activity. Some restoration work was done in 1880 when the new church, at the head of the hause, was built. In the churchyard there is a very old yew tree, itself several centuries old. They were said to be planted to supply wood for long-bows. But the evergreen yew was also planted in churchyards as a symbol of everlasting life. Yew trees can live on for many centuries. The sticky berries are much enjoyed by birds but are reckoned to be poisonous to humans. The foliage, when cut and partly withered, is dangerous to cattle.

On leaving the church turn right and follow the road. There is a fine sycamore on the left. At the road junction walk on. The old school is down on the left. Follow the road up to your starting point.

Seldom Seen is seldom visited; that is why it is called Seldom Seen.
Seldom Seen is in fact a row of cottages in secluded Glencoynedale
on the western side of the head of Ullswater. A walk up this dale can
be highly recommended. The return journey is through farm land on
which dogs must be kept on leash.

Park at Stybarrow Crag. This is half a mile north of Glenridding.
On either side of the parking area, which is on the opposite side to
the lake, are warning signs "Beware Falling Stones". What one is
supposed to do about the falling stones is a mystery but the possibility
that you may return to your parked car to find it crushed to pulp is
remote, I think. The parking area is restricted and on busy days
you may not find a place. There are one or two other parking spaces
farther north. (But do not block gateways.)

Cross the road to the lake shore — which is owned by the National
Trust and is open to the public — and walk on northwards away
from Glenridding. After half a mile the steepness down to the lake
will force you along a path close to the road. Look for a stone
track opposite, cross carefully and go onto it. There are two private
drives leading from it; one left and one right. Go right on. You are
walking on a rough track with Glencoyne Woods towering up the
hillside above you. There are some fine old trees hereabouts, most of
those near the track being sycamores. This is not a native tree,
but is very common and seeds readily. There are some large boulders
which have come from the heights at one time. (And may have
inspired the notices on the main road?) There are some fine views
down Ullswater, particularly from near the two seats. Farther on
there are some coppiced oaks, and a wych elm or two over the wall
to the right. Glencoyne Farm, which is crowned by the old cylindrical
type lakeland chimney stacks, is below on the right.

At the row of cottages on Seldom Seen you turn left up the
old path under the pine trees. The crag ahead is Black Crag,
the northern wall of Sheffield Pike. When you reach a point
where the path comes close to the wall near a group of oak trees,
look down Ullswater again. Above on the left is a larch tree which
has picked up stones as it has grown and has them embedded in
its trunk. Continue on along the path following the wall. You must
presently duck below the boughs of a thick-trunked sweet chestnut.
Go over the stile then immediately afterwards turn right and go
through the gate. Pick your way carefully among the loose stones
beyond, then follow the wall on the right, round the corner onto a
grassy path. There is now an open view down Ullswater. The wall
is on the right for a time, then the path goes downhill away from it

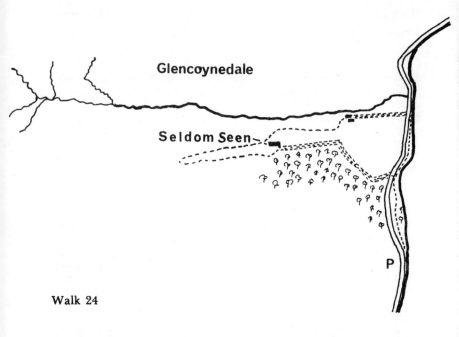

Glencoynedale

Seldom Seen

Walk 24

towards the cottages of Seldom Seen. The grass is rather steep in
places and care should be taken.

Do not go right on to Seldom Seen but head to the front (left)
of it, and pick up the path between the property and Glencoyne
Beck. The beck is the boundary between Cumberland and Westmorland; you are of course on the Westmorland side. The trees
thriving around here are mainly alders, which prefer wet ground.
You go through a gate onto farmland. The path is not clear on the
grass but it follows an obvious natural line. It goes by a lone ash
tree growing by what was a gap in a wall, now tumbledown. Another
broken wall is shortly passed through by another ash tree; then the
path goes left towards the chimneys of Glencoyne Farm. The sheep
pens below look a little complicated in design. In fact, they have
been carefully designed for sheep handling with the least effort.
This farm, which is owned by the National Trust, is an important
one, and a show-piece. The path goes towards the gable end of the
farmhouse, then left through a gate. Go through the farmyard and
on down the track to the main road.

Cross the road with care and walk along the lake shore. A raised
path is then reached which follows the road and the lake shore.
You soon reach your car again. (Flattened, or covered in fallen
stones?)

80

There are many Grisedales or Grizedales in the Lake District. They date from the early Norse settlers who habitually had a special part of a valley, or a whole valley, for pasturing swine; Grise means pig or boar. The best known Grisedale is an eastern-facing valley at the foot of Helvellyn. It is a typical glacial valley — cut out by retreating ice at the end of the ice age. Unlike many of the valleys in the high fells one can enjoy an interesting round walk in it, as two good tracks go up on either side of its beck. From its northern track starts the popular Striding Edge path for Helvellyn. A good many of the walkers on this path have no idea what they are in for, and fondly imagine that the gap in the wall on the skyline is near the mountain summit. It is less than half way! Only novices can make such a mistake. But a very great many novices attempt Helvellyn by this route as accident records show — but that is another story. Not for you the crowded struggle to the summit, but a quiet walk in a green valley cupped in great crags.

The tracks are good and for the most part easily seen though they may be wet in places after bad weather.

Park your car in Patterdale. At busy times this may not be easy. If you have difficulty you could park in the more accommodating village of Glenridding and do two walks in one — walk 26 to Keldas, joining this route passing by Lanty's Tarn. Starting at Patterdale walk towards Glenridding past the church. Just after this a narrow surfaced lane goes off to the left past the playing fields. Take this. The lane climbs through trees and past entrance drives. The author counted sixteen different species of broad-leaf trees. At the top of this lane go through the gate. There is a field on the right. The lane goes through a gate at the end of this field, but do not go this way, turn right on the stone track by the wall and walk to the bridge.

Go over the bridge and right up the hill. Go through the gate at the top and onto the Striding Edge track, but instead of going up it, turn left onto an indistinct path through the bracken. In mid-summer this bracken may be somewhat dense. As you proceed you might almost expect a rhinoceros to burst through the jungle, or a pith-helmeted gentleman making the assumption that you are Doctor Livingstone. But you soon leave it straight ahead onto a reasonable path, on grass. Go through a pretty iron gate. Below on the left among a grove of trees is a farm, Braesteads. Then there is a pleasant grove of Scots pine. The path is plainer now.

Several becks have to be forded. (These were once culverted under the track.) A wood is soon below to the left. This is mainly of Scots pine with some hardwoods. There are some spruces among the

81

plantings but they do not seem to have done well. Go through the iron gate. As you go on you will see a good number of large boulders which have mainly fallen from the crags above. But some of the half-buried ones may be seen to have glacial scratches on them where hard rocks were pressed and pushed along them by retreating ice. The hump of a fell on the left is Birks, part of the summit ridge of St. Sunday Crag which is straight ahead and to the left of the dip at the valley summit.

Cross the wooden bridge. Above on the right is Nethermost Cove. Typically of glacial valleys this is a "hanging valley" above the main one, the ice having scooped out a pocket in its descent. Beyond this point the track goes through a wall for the summit of the pass. Go through the gate in this wall, but immediately afterwards go left and follow the wall down, then left, around its corner, to a foot-bridge. Turn right and cross this bridge. Go forward, keeping to the higher ground to pass the bog, then bear left to join the track going down the valley again. Ford two streams.

There is soon a mixed wood on the left (Crossing Plantation) and the path becomes wider. Leaving the wood you go through a gate near a little "hog-house" (pronounced "ogguss") a little barn. Go through another gate. There is now a wood on the right, another mixture of hardwoods with larch. Wild cherry trees seem to be in favour here. Go through another gate by the farm which the wood protects (Elmhow). Go through another gate and the track wanders pleasantly through fields. If you look left you will probably see walkers struggling up the fell-side path to Striding Edge. Through another gate and the track goes very pleasantly alongside the beck. At the next gate the road is better surfaced. The old barn on the right, among the grove of old trees, makes a pretty picture. Go through the gate and you are back on the lane by which you started.

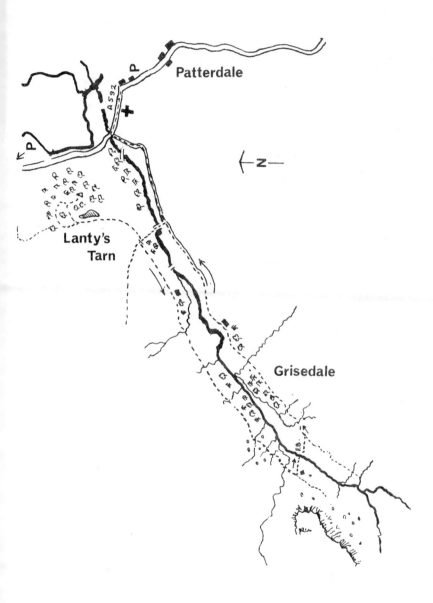

Patterdale

Lanty's
Tarn

Grisedale

Walks 25 and 26

A favourite viewpoint beloved of photographers overlooks Ullswater
from a high spot between Glenridding and Patterdale. The picture
of the lake, framed by a foreground of Scots pines, has appeared in
books and on calendars, and has raised innumerable "oohs!" at slide
shows no doubt. The high point has the odd name of "Keldas".
The path to it is steep, but short. Some will need to take it slowly.
The walk starts at Glenridding Car Park.

Leave the car park by the entrance, turn right, cross the bridge,
and turn right again to follow the lane past the shops. Go on past
the hall and through the buildings. Go through the gate and on up a
stone track. Presently the track climbs through some deciduous trees.
There should be a slate sign directing walkers to Helvellyn. Keep left.
After the old cottages the path goes left over a footbridge and
through a gate. You must then trudge up the steepening incline
between alder trees. If you need to take breath look backwards. The
valley you are leaving is Glenridding, and at its top was once a very
profitable lead mine, a few buildings of which still remain.

In 1927 there was a catastrophe for the village of Glenridding
when a dam, supplying water for the mine, and high up the valley,
burst during a heavy storm. It did great damage but miraculously
there were no casualties. The only sigh remaining is the stone
headlar ', formed by flood debris, which thrusts into Ullswater at the
steamer pier.

Go over stile and continue up steep hill. Panters can now look back
at Ullswater. The path levels out. In front there is a gate. The path
to Keldas does not go through this gate, but turns left just before it,
through an old gateway in a wall and up through Scots pines.

Go slightly left through another gap in a broken wall. Go forward
and at a point where the path begins to fall a little by the second
of two pine trees, turn right and head for the cairn on the little
summit. Go by way of the group of pine trees. As you reach this
group a marvellous view down Ullswater opens up. Turn right and
head upwards and go to the sharp-pointed cairn. Sheffield Pike,
over the Glenridding valley, remains the most impressive point from
this view. Looking back over the tarn, St. Sunday Crag is the nearest
high point over Grisedale. To the right of the valley head, and
commanding the head, is Dollywaggon Pike (2,810 feet) which is
Helvellyn's southernmost spur. The summit of Helvellyn is obscured
to the right of this, but you should see the approach path to Striding
Edge, the ridge which heads for it from this side. Under Sheffield
Pike at the head of the valley from Glenridding can be seen the
remains of the lead mine. The old "tailing dam" — the great bank

of mine waste — to the right of the workings, has been sown with grass to hide the scars, and is partly successful.

Walk back to the group of pines you just left. Then bear right to the tree-crowned knoll, towards the lake. (The path is rather indistinct.) There is a lovely pine on this summit. Go beyond it towards the lake, bearing left slightly. There are several good viewpoints. Another point is reached by going back towards the summit, but when you descend into the hollow before it, turn right. A faint path leads onto a bracken-covered knoll. Go forward and left onto the next knoll. The chestnut trees on the left are a glorious colour in the autumn. The steamer pier at Glenridding can be clearly seen. The large hump of a fell the other side of the lake is Place Fell. A crag from it dominates the point — Silver Point. With binoculars at any time other than at the height of the summer season, you might be able to see red deer on the side of Place Fell, as they wander over here from Martindale Deer Forest three miles beyond.

Return to the path by which you approached. Before descending by the route you came, a slight diversion through the gate reveals a pretty tarn — Lanty's Tarn. (To join Walk 25 from here continue past the tarn and the path is joined by the gate on the Striding Edge track.)

___

As you go southwards beyond the head of Ullswater the heights of Fairfield and Caudale Moor crowd about the cleft of Kirkstone Pass —the highest road in the Lake District (1,489 feet). Before reaching Ullswater the becks which race down the craggy steeps fall into a little hollow. This is Brothers Water, passed by thousands of motorists but seldom admired except from a moving window. The western banks are in the care of the National Trust and there is free access to the lake. A walk around the lake is possible by using permissive footpaths and rights of way. Dogs must be on leads.

Drive southwards beyond the head of Ullswater and after about 2½ miles the road turns left and there is a large lay-by and an AA box. Park on this lay-by. Walk on along the roadside footpath and at the road junction in the corner of the bend turn right along the main road. The footpath is on the left of the road; then when this finishes look across the road and you will see a wooden kissing-gate leading into the lakeside field. Cross with care and go through this. Go left along the lake shore. This is a permissive path and it continues along the shore to the wall at the end of the lake. Follow the wall to the road above. Walk along the road for about 70 yards only, then cross carefully, ascend steps, and go through the kissing-gate. Follow path with the fence through gates to just beyond the Brotherswater Hotel. Then leave the path sharp right through kissing-gate, and cross carefully to the hotel. From the hotel yard a public right of way goes down through the camping field. The great cleft of Dovedale is on the left. Follow track down and go through the gate. Cross the wooden bridge. The peak on the far right-hand side of the head of Dovedale is Hart Crag (2,698 feet); Dove Crag is to the left of this. Left of this and nearer to you is a "dodd", a grassy fell separated from the main fell. It is High Hartsop Dodd, a mere 1,702 feet, but is in a commanding position. Go through another gate, turn left, and then go right round the back of the Hall. A track is joined and you follow it, right.

Go through gate where there is a fine sycamore on the right. After a second sycamore on the right, look up the bank left and see a fine wych elm. This elm is commoner in the north than its near relative, the smooth leaved elm which is more typical as a large field tree in the lowlands of the south of England. Elm timber is tough and durable and makes fine furniture. It has always been used for coffin making too. Perhaps this fact, plus the habit of the elm of dropping branches without warning—sometimes with disastrous results to anyone who has sat under it, built under it, or parked their new car under it—and probably also to the traditional belief that "elm wood

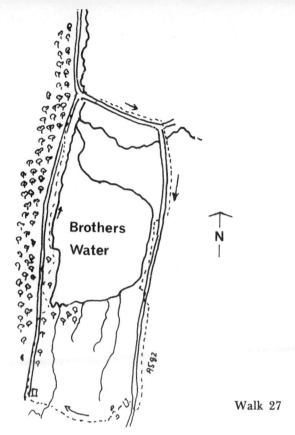

Brothers

Water

N

Walk 27

burns cold", has given rise to the long held legend that "the elm it loveth not mankind". There is another elm on the right just over the fence and further on.

Go through the gateway. Note how the ash tree on the right has wrapped itself around the steel fence. You soon approach the shore of Brothers Water again and here is a pleasant place to linger. Looking across one can see on the far fells two pikes, looking like miniatures of the famous Langdale Pikes. These are the Angle Tarn Pikes.

You can stroll along the lake shore for a distance, but then one is forced by the rough ground to walk up the bank to the lane again. The wood up on the left has been scheduled as an Area of Special Scientific Interest as it is a very typical natural wood, mainly oak with a lot of hazel, but mixed in naturally are rowan, ash, hawthorn and holly. The lake shore is accessible again further on, and as all this area, including the wood, belongs to the National Trust you are free to wander and linger—so long as it is remembered that you have responsibilities as well as rights. The lane, overhung with many hazels, leads back to the lay-by where you left the car.

Hayeswater is a mountain tarn with its level slightly raised by a
dam, as it is a reservoir. However if you can close your eyes to the
minor mess at the dam, the water's setting amongst fierce crags gives
it a wild and haunting appearance. It is well worth the modest
climb. A walk to the lake and back is only 2½ miles — but make
allowance for the climb of about 750 feet. A circuit of the water
makes it four miles, but good footwear is essential. The paths are
good to the tarn, but boggy around it.

Travelling south from Patterdale the road approaches Brothers
Water and bends left to pass it. There is an AA box at the bend.
Shortly from this point there is a straight stretch of road and a sharp
bend right from Kirkstone; but opening directly on this bend and
right ahead of you is a minor road into the village of Hartsop. Take
this road and drive carefully through the village, following the road
upwards and right until a car parking area is reached on the right.
Park here.

Leave the car park, go ahead through the gate and on up the stony
track. Go through another gate and immediately afterwards fork
right. Cross the beck by the concrete footbridge, go forward and turn
left before you get to the gap in the wall. Follow the wall up.
The path rises, then goes right through a wall gap towards a barn
and then turns left to climb the fell between walls. The barn on
the right is quite charming; traditional style with its roof crowned
with ferns, and framed in sycamores. The path steepens but it is
pleasant and green underfoot. There is a view back to Brothers
Water. Go through the gate.

When the track levels out a little there is a fine view of waterfalls below; they are especially good after heavy rain. As the track
comes nearer to the beck it begins to get rougher. Below in the beck
there are some very nice "dubs" — smooth hollows in the rocky beck
bed, sculptured by current-borne pebbles and gravel. After the
shapes that nature has made, what man has thrown up at the dam is
an atrocity! There is a small building like a mini public lavatory.
Pretend it is not there. The "Private" notices which also disfigure
this point, indicate only that the fishing is private. Forward beyond
the dam is a rounded knoll which gives a good view of the little
lake. If there is a wind blowing there are one or two sheltered
coves where one can picnic in comfort. But *please* take your litter
back. The author removed a large quantity of filth from this area
when compiling these notes. Odd that people can carry full cans and
bottles up — but are too lazy to carry the empty ones down.

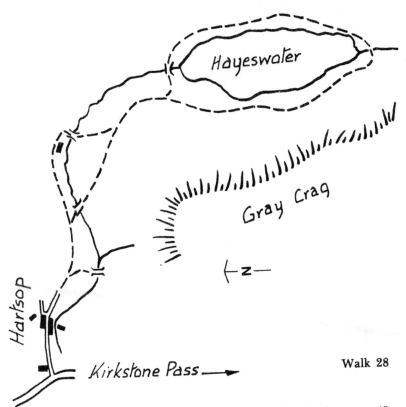

Hayeswater

Gray Crag

Hartsop

Kirkstone Pass ——►

Walk 28

The walk round the tarn from here should take between 45 minutes and an hour. There is some wetness to cross at the far end but the circumambulation is otherwise enjoyable. As you go up the valley you can see some splendid examples of moraines; rounded hills which are really deposits of worn rocks scooped out of the heights by the retreating ice of the last ice age, and left behind when the ice melted. The valley is a "hanging valley" bored out of the mountain side by the pressure of ice.

There is a reasonable path all the way to the head of the tarn, but to cross to the other side on reaching the head there is a mass of rushy wet ground. To avoid the worst of this, walk right on up to the moraine heaps before turning left. The view up the craggy valley head of Thornthwaite, shut in by the great walls of High Street and with Gray Crag on the right, is dramatic. Pick your way along the pathless green, crossing the little becks and going through the old wall by one of the gaps. Make for the moraines on the far side before turning down the lake again, and a narrow path will be picked up. This goes close to the lake shore and there are some pretty shingle beaches.

89

On reaching the dam again leave by the path on which you arrived. If you wish, you can descend all the way by this very easy path, but there is an alternative way with an initial steepness. Watch for the waterworks building on the right of the beck below. On seeing it you should also see a footbridge to it, with a steep path leading there from the path on which you walk. Go down, cross the footbridge, and cross the slate-stepped stile just below it. You pass the waterworks buildings and a good track is joined; follow it down past the waterworks litter. As you go down the track across the valley you can see the barn which you passed on the way up. It fits into the scene perfectly. The valley head behind it, wild and craggy, leads up into Thresthwaite Cove. Go through the gate. As you descend to the next gate, look at the wall on your right. Each stone has been laid carefully to fit — like a three-dimensional jig-saw. But the size of some of those stones, carefully turned and placed, makes one wonder at the strength of the man who made it. From this point you are soon back at the car park.

Lowther Castle is only a facade. The early 19th century building by Robert Smirke was gutted, being far too expensive to maintain. It is now nothing more than a picturesque decoration to the Lowther Estate. The present Earl of Lonsdale has opened up part of the estate as a wildlife park which is very popular. Other parts of the estate offer away-from-it-all pleasant walks. This walk is one suggestion. In parts it is over grass which may be wet. It starts at Askham. This is reached from Pooley Bridge at the foot of Ullswater by leaving the village by the B5320 Eamont Bridge and Penrith road. After one mile turn right onto a minor road and Askham is reached in two and a half miles. At the centre of the pretty village turn left down the hill and park near the church. (If a service is in progress avoid making a noise).

Walk down to the bridge over the river Lowther, cross it, then turn right up the track which climbs gently through the wood. At the top it becomes a path and turns left through a plantation of spruces then joins a drive. Turn left on it. As this drive bends right you have a view of Lowther Castle. Go over the cattle grid and the track bends left. On the left is a long avenue of oaks. The drive forks; take the left hand lane. This is not strictly speaking, a right of way; but is permissive and is only a short stretch. There are good views of the castle as you retreat from its proximity. Go through the gate at the end of the lane and — very important — close it after you. Turn left and walk along the grass verge. You cross the avenue which you observed from the castle end. In between the oaks some limes as well as sycamores have been planted. You are heading for the chapel. It can be seen on the right and is well worth a visit, so go through the iron wicket gate to it. The Lowther vault is on the left.

In the chapel, part of the nave dates from 1170, the stone columns being oddly carved with grotesque beasts. One of them was never finished. The octagonal columns were put in in the 13th century. The lower part of the tower also is from the same date. The middle portion is 17th century and the top stage was built when the whole of the building was restored later in the same century by Sir John Lowther. There are some stone fragments which pre-date the church. Literature on the history of the building is on display.

Leave the chapel and walk back along the grass verge the way you came for a short distance. A road is soon seen going off to the left. The "No entry" and "Private" notices refer to traffic so there is a right of way on foot. Cross the cattlegrid. The road forks; bear left. The road ends at a bridge over the river. In fact, you have a choice of two bridges. The older and attractive arch bridge has

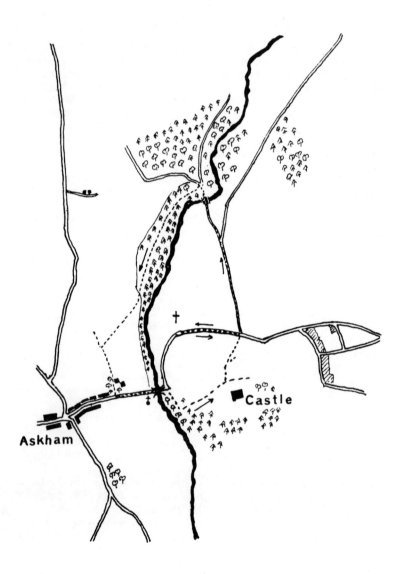

Castle

Askham

Walk 29

become unsafe for traffic but can be crossed, with little risk, on foot. The newer bridge is safe and purely functional. Go forward along the road from the bridge. At the road fork turn left. Almost immediately there is a path left going up through the wood. Take this path, through spruces. The path is joined by another from the right. Keep on. The path narrows through undergrowth. If necessary, make a short detour right, then left to the end of a fence. The path can now be seen running parallel with the river. Keep well to the right on the path as there is a certain amount of erosion on its left. You come to a group of fine pine trees. At the time of writing there is a good view from here over to the castle but one supposes that in time the trees below are going to grow up and ɔbscure it. A little gully is crossed and there is a fairly steep bank to climb. Just after this gully you cross the line of the castle again, but at this end it has been planted up.

You now walk through a ride among spruce trees. Presently you should see that you are walking parallel to a wall on the right. For a time the trees close in and the path narrows but then the way gets near to the wall. You here turn sharp right and go through a gate into a field. Gorward and left you will see a gate at the far side. Make for this. Go through the gate and you are on a green track. Turn left. Presently this track passes by Askham Hall. Go through gate and across the yard, bearing right at the end, and along the track between the wall and the trees. This brings you out to the village street again and you turn left to the church.

Shap is something of a bleak place and not at all characteristic of the
Lake District, but perhaps reminding one of the "Wuthering Height"
area of the Pennines. Its austere fells apparently had some effect on
John Ruskin, the connoisseur of highland scenery, because when
he wrote about some remote spot in the Alps which he admired
he said, "Ever since I passed Shap Fells, when a child, I have had an
excessive love for this kind of desolation." Something about the area
seems to inspire religious feelings. In neolithic times there was
religious activity here indicated by a number of significant stones,
although the building of the village and the railway has confused
the pattern of them. Shap Abbey, almost hidden on the banks
of the Lowther, was founded in 1150 and built by Premonstrat-
ensians — usually known as the "White Canons" by reason of their
dress. The abbey was surrendered in 1540 and many of the stones
were taken for the building of nearby Lowther Castle. All that
remains of substance is the tower. However, the ruin is under the
care of the Ministry of Works and it is possible to gain a good
impression of the original structure by following their excavations. A
resident keeper has literature.

The walk, which goes first by a 16th century chapel at Keld,
is largely over fields and during or after rain, or after a heavy dew,
Wellington boots might be a good idea. Park the car in Shap village,
on the main A6, Penrith to Kendal road. This is a quiet road now
the motorway is open. At one time Shap was a constant roar of north-
and south-bound traffic; now it is almost sleepy. First impressions of
Shap are usually depressing, yet some holidaymakers, admitting to
this first impression, return to the village year after year. Maybe it
is the air — the place is at over 800 feet.

Walk along the main street (the A6) towards Kendal. Look for the
Methodist Church right, with the gates of the park opposite. Just
after this on the left is Croft Avenue. Almost opposite is a farm gate
with a small wooden gate alongside it. Go through this. Go forward
between walls and past the farmyard, and turn left through the gate.
Then go right to follow the wall which is now on your right. Go over
the stile at the end. Now go forward and right across the next field.
If this section is indistinct the stile you are aiming for is in the middle
of the row of trees at the far side. Go over this, and then over the
stile opposite and across into the next field. If again the way is
indistinct make for a point some way to the left of the gate and tree
ahead. Just when you reach the wall you should see a stile. Do not
go over this, however, but turn left and follow the path by the wall.
Go over another stile and continue following the wall until you are

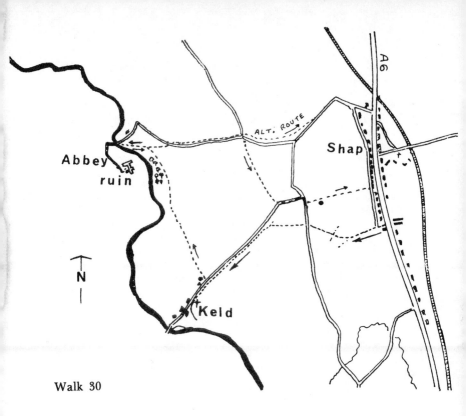

Walk 30

getting near to a wall corner at the end. Look for a stile on your right into the road. Go over this and turn left into the village.

"Keld" is a common name in the Lake District. It means "spring" or "well" and Keld Chapel is reached immediately in the middle of the Y-junction. In the care of the National Trust, it is a very simple rural place of worship, 400 years old. The fireplace is a little younger. The key can be had at a nearby cottage and one can hardly enter the chapel without feeling the atmosphere of years and years of worship. At one time there was a local tradition that there was a secret passage from the chapel to the abbey but no-one has explained why.

Walk away from the village by the route you entered but this time after the farm and a barn on the left look for a stone step-stile. (This is at about 100 yards.) Go over this and follow the wall which is on your right. Go forward at the wall corner to another stile in the wall in front. Follow the wall which is now on your left for about 100 yards and then there is a stile on your left. Go over it and then bear right, following a less distinct path roughly parallel with the wall. You reach a stile on the left of a gate. Go over it and follow the wall which is now on your left. Suddenly the broken tower of the Abbey appears dramatically on the left below. Continue to the next stile. Then bear left with care down to the concrete track near the river. Go on across the bridge and follow the track to the Abbey. (If the information hut is unoccupied you may find the curator at his home near the car park.) The site is so well kept you will want to linger.

To continue the walk leave by the bank down which you arrived. This time, however, go forward and up to the gate in the distance. A stile will be seen through the wall on its left. Go over this. There is a last view of the Abbey from its top. Go along the field-side following the wall. There is a large boulder stile in the wall at the left at the end. Go over it and right to the road junction. Take the path on the right between the walls. If you do this walk in summer, Cranesbill, a wild blue geranium, grows almost shoulder high and the path is fragrant with meadowsweet, also very high. However, there are nettles, too, so watch out. Children may have to be carried. People wearing shorts may like to take an alternative, though less interesting, route. (See below.) Large specimens of the mauve flower, field scabious, also grow along this way; and chin-high giant bellflower (campanula latifolia), a northern plant not found in the south of England. The growth becomes thicker, but suddenly there is an improvement. The path becomes a track and you join a road. Turn left. At the road bend turn right to go between walls again on another path. Shortly there is a stile through the wall on the left. Go over this.

Follow the wall on your left. There is a strange lone boulder on your right which must have been put there by human agency in neolithic times. It is the Goggleby Stone. There are quite a few such stones in the area, some of them called "Thunder Stones". Go over two more stiles and forward, and the village will soon be seen. Go through two gates and onto the village street.

To walk the alternative route from the road junction mentioned above take the path alongside the field, which follows the road on towards the village. There is a stile opposite the one from which you emerged out of the last field. Go over a stile, and the road is rejoined at a gate and leads on to the village.

If you enjoy looking at old churches, the parish church of St. Michael's should also be visited. It is Norman, and is on the east side of the A6.